Hello, Beautiful!

FINALLY LOVE YOURSELF JUST AS YOU ARE

An Interactive Devotional Journal for Women

Praise for *Hello, Beautiful!*

This delightful book skillfully reminds us that while true beauty radiates from a woman's inner spirit, most of us have struggled with feelings of inadequacy, failure, and condemnation that cloud our radiance. Using poignant humor, personal stories, powerful Scriptures, and practical tips, the authors highlight eternal truths that can set women free from emotional bondage. Don't miss this enjoyable read and its uplifting takeaway value.

—**Diana Savage**, author, speaker, and principal at Savage Creative Services, LLC, www.DianaSavage.com

If you've never thought of yourself as beautiful, Jeanette Levellie and Beth Gormong will open your eyes to God's beauty within you on each page of *Hello, Beautiful!* Through real-life stories, the authors inspire you to trust God for the courage to reach new heights of maturity by accepting yourself and appreciating how wonderfully he made each of us—all different but each of us unique and special. You will never look in the mirror the same way again because you will see the beauty of God in yourself. You'll also see the beauty in those you encounter daily. Some chapters bring tears, others joy, but all impart spiritual insight. *Hello, Beautiful!* helps us understand how God wants to show off his power through our less-than-perfect selves.

—**Peggy Cunningham**, author of *Shape Your Soul: 31 Exercises for Faith that Moves Mountains.* www.PeggyCunningham.com

Okay, I may not be "beautiful," but I thoroughly enjoyed editing Jeanette and Beth's latest book. It's an encouraging and entertaining devotional for both genders. So, for guys to benefit as well, just substitute *handsome* every time you see the word *beautiful*.

—**James N. Watkins**, author, speaker, threat to society

"The fairest of them all" is not just in fairy tales. Jeanette Levellie and Beth Gormong will help you see yourself through the eyes of the Father. Be ready to discover the beautiful Spirit that reflects you.

—**Teri Bennett**, author/teacher

I work with Jeanette and very much enjoy her sunny soul. Her books and articles bring a smile to my face, a chuckle to my belly, and sometimes tears to my eyes. Jeanette writes from the heart and through her great and abiding love for God in Jesus Christ. I recommend her and Beth Gormong's book *Hello, Beautiful!* The devotions are heartfelt and help readers continue on their spiritual journey. I also appreciate the interactive portions encouraging us to reflect and do, not merely read and move on.

—**Laurie Williams**, co-pastor of The Presbyterian Church, Paris, IL

In this collection of personal experiences, Jeanette Levellie and Beth Gormong offer quiet wisdom, Godly perspective, and delightful encouragement. Their touching stories will feed hungry souls in this busy, stress-filled world, gently reviving hearts and minds.

—**Karen Lange**, freelance writer, editor, and author

Facing a mirror daily can be unsettling, even startling, but Jeanette Levellie and Beth Gormong show women how to face reality and see themselves how beautifully and uniquely the Lord created them. What encouragement!

—**Susan Hayhurst**, freelance writer

HELLO, BEAUTIFUL!

FINALLY LOVE YOURSELF JUST AS YOU ARE

An Interactive Devotional Journal for Women

JEANETTE LEVELLIE

BETH GORMONG

COLORING PAGES BY BETH GORMONG

PUBLISHING THE POSITIVE

ELK LAKE PUBLISHING INC
Plymouth, Massachusetts

Library of Congress Data:

Names: Levellie, Jeanette and Gormong, Beth (Jeanette Levellie and Beth Gormong)

Hello, Beautiful! / Jeanette Levellie, Beth Gormong

170 p. 23cm × 15cm (9in × 6 in.)

Description:

Identifiers: ISBN-13: 978-1-950051-30-4 (Trade) | 978-1-950051-31-1 (POD) |

978-1-950051-32-8 (e-book)

Key Words: self-esteem, self-confidence, devotional, inspirational, women, Christian living, self-image

LCCN: 2019937358 Nonfiction

DEDICATION

To my daughters, Jaena, Johanna, and Jessica, because you believe in me. Your strength makes me strong.
—Beth

To the extraordinary women who have most shown me God's beauty: Marie Adams, Beth Gormong, Doris Kidgell, Beverly Mathieson, Kathy Nobilione, Nancy Sanchez, Diana Savage, Judy Smith, Dee Stark, Joyce Tomson, and my grandmother, Viola Tomson, who shines from heaven.

Thank you.
—Jeanette

CONTENTS

Praise for *Hello, Beautiful!* ii
Acknowledgments. xiii
Introduction 1
1. Hello, Beautiful! 3
2. The Best Daddy. 7
3. Zits, Faults and All 11
4. A New Name 15
5. Jesus's Reading Material. 17
6. Quit Punishing Yourself 21
7. Ornery, Ugly, or Kind to Yourself?. 25
8. Christmas Card Kindness 29
9. The Apology 31
10. Have Some Dirt, Please. 35
11. Perfume-mania 37
12. Cooking Up Confidence 41
13. All Gods on This Shelf. 45
14. Trade a Trouble 49
15. A Few of My Favorite Things. .53
16. Courage through Failure 57
17. Dream a Big Dream with Me .61
18. God Likes Farmers 65
19. Chatterbox or Cheerleader 69
20. Created with a Purpose 73
21. Mighty Peace. 77
22. Dropping the Bell 81
23. I Promise. 85
24. Hiding in Plain Sight 89
25. One Step at a Time 91
26. Broken Sheep 95

27. Today's Joy 97
28. Never Forgotten 99
29. Encourage Me, Please! 103
30. Princess 105
31. Suit Yourself 109
32. Running with Grief 111
33. Bruised but Beautiful 113
34. Trying Too Hard 117
35. Grace and Glory 121
36. Stolen Dreams 125
37. You Love Me Just as I Am 127
38. Puddles of Gold 131
39. There All the Time 135
40. You Are Stronger Than You Think 139
Bonus Chapter: Hope for a Poor Self-image 143
About Jeanette Levellie 153
About Beth Gormong 155

ACKNOWLEDGMENTS

To the Holy Spirit, who comforts, encourages, and helps me write, I love and appreciate you.

To my prayer partners, who have gone to God's throne on my behalf, I'd be sunk without you: Beth Gormong, Karen Lange, Cecelia Lester, Bev Mathieson, Cecil Murphey, Kathy Nobilione, Diana Flegal, Gloria Penwell, Cammie Quinn, Diana Savage, Dee Stark, and James Watkins. I appreciate your love shown in time spent interceding for me and my family.

To my coauthor, Beth Gormong, you are one brave lady! Your gracious spirit helps me stand up on the inside. From you, I've learned listening is the best way to love someone. Thank you for that gift.

To my husband, Kevin, always praying, forgiving, and showing me what Jesus looks like, you are the center of my heart. I appreciate you supporting my dreams, sometimes believing in me more than I do in myself. Wow.

And to you who are reading this book, thank you. May you know and believe the love God has for you, you beautiful lady.

—Jeanette

I would like to thank Jeanette Levellie, my coauthor, for her patience, knowledge, and wisdom throughout the writing of this book. I owe her a debt I won't ever be able to pay for pushing me out of my comfortable, but unsatisfying life to pursue this writing project. Without her, I'd still be scribbling in my journal and wishing my dreams away.

I want to thank my college writing professors: Dr. Marjorie Elder, for seeing a glimpse of possibility in those first writing assignments, and Dr. Mary Brown, for the hours of instruction and encouragement that lit a passion for the written word in my brain and heart.

I would like to thank my husband, Jeff, for believing in my talent, and encouraging me to spend hours in my upstairs writing studio. I'm especially thankful that he doesn't complain too much that the bathroom goes unmopped, the dishes undone, and the ironing sent out to the drycleaners so I can spend the precious time needed to follow my heart's desire.

I would like to thank my three daughters, Jaena, Johanna, and Jessica for seeing me as a person, not just their mom, and for inspiring me to make and complete goals. You've grown up to be independent and strong women. Thank you for letting me share your stories with the world.

Most importantly, I'm thankful to God, my Savior, who loves me unconditionally even when I doubt my lovability, who promised he would never leave me or forsake me and who has guided me over the mountains and through the valleys.

—Beth

To our publisher, Deb Haggerty, and our editors, Jeanne Marie Leach, James Watkins, and Diana Savage, thanks for making us look and sound better than we really are.

—Beth and Jeanette

INTRODUCTION

Our parents and church leaders taught us when we were children that we could find the secret to fulfillment in the acrostic JOY (Jesus, others, yourself). If you put Jesus first, others next, and yourself last, your life would brim with happiness. In theory, this sounds like the humility and servanthood Jesus taught and practiced. Yet, we've all known women who've put their husbands, children, and friends ahead of their own genuine need for value and love, only to end up mentally burned out, physically beaten up, or emotionally bruised.

There is a better way to a life of joy: *love yourself.*

Jesus told us in Luke 10:27 that one of the greatest commandments is to *love your neighbor as yourself.* The writers of Romans, Galatians, and James reiterate Jesus's truth by telling us that if we love our neighbor as ourselves, we are fulfilling the law and doing right. (Romans 5:14, Galatians 13:9, James 2:8). So, the principle to love ourselves in order to love others comes from God's Word.

Yet, we see low self-esteem and even self-hatred around us every day. Women who can find something good to say about anyone but themselves. Women who mistakenly think they're acting in sinful pride if they say, "I'm happy that I refused to gossip today when I had the opportunity." Women who starve themselves to look like the latest fashion model or to fit into a smaller size of pants. Women so beaten down by society—and even by well-meaning but mistaken church leaders—that they like very little about themselves.

That's why we wrote this book.

We want to see women take Jesus's words seriously enough that they are set free from erroneously thinking they are never good enough, that they must be perfect to be loved, and that skinny equals pretty. We want to help women break free of faulty teaching and bask in the reality of God's high esteem and deep love for them. To love themselves without guilt or shame. If women catch the Master's meaning of true love—starting with themselves—as precious ones made in God's image, they'll hold their heads up high. The gleam in their eyes will reflect the love they've willingly received from God. And there will be no end to what they can achieve to make this world a lovelier place.

Because once women realize a truth and act on it, no power on earth or in hell can stop them.

Are you ready to start an adventure that will shake up the old ideas you've had about how God sees you and how you should see yourself? Are you ready to find out how greatly you are valued by your heavenly Father? Are you brave enough to learn that you're allowed to finally look in the mirror and say—regardless of your size, shape, or social standing—"Hello, Beautiful!"?

1

Hello, Beautiful!

How precious to me are your thoughts, O God! How vast is the sum of them! Were I to count them, they would outnumber the grains of sand. (Psalm 139:17-18)

The craziness started when I volunteered to present a program for the weight loss club I attend. I devised a game for the members to play based on the popular game, *Scattergories*®, naming my version "Low Fategories."

For prizes, I created fridge magnets with colorful, glittery butterflies to attract attention and to motivate us to stay with our healthy eating plans. I made a total of six designs, with sayings like "No is not a four-letter word," "I can do this," and "Keep a watch over my mouth, Lord." But I was shocked at the response to the ones that said "Hello, Beautiful."

After the meeting, the magnets I thought were the most encouraging still sat on the eight-foot table like unadopted shelter puppies. Although the members enthused over the other designs, not one person took a "Hello, Beautiful" magnet. I gathered them up, shoved them in my tote, and gave the rest of them to my two friends at work, both of whom regifted them to relatives. No one wanted to decorate their own fridge with "Hello, Beautiful."

What was wrong with these people, Lord? Why didn't they like themselves enough to have even a sparkly butterfly tell them they're beautiful?

But when I looked at my own fridge, I noticed I'd put a "No is not a four-letter word" magnet among the love notes from my kids, jokes, and photos of my grandbabies. Even I couldn't take a dose of my own encouragement. I choked on the word *beautiful* in connection with myself.

Perhaps we're afraid—even in the privacy of our own homes—to come across as arrogant. Or perhaps it's because our society equates beauty with outward appearance only.

Even though the Creator of the universe made us in his image (Genesis 1:26), we've believed the lie that unless our bodies are perfectly shaped and toned, we are less than attractive or valuable. We're quick to tell our friends and coworkers how great they look or how special they make us feel. But we can't say it in our own mirror or on our own fridge.

I decided to help those around me—and myself—get a glimpse of the beauty God put inside us. So, we weren't ready to think our bodies were pretty. But could we start from the inside and work our way out, changing our self-image one baby step at a time?

I began to hand out genuine compliments to those around me. I told the cashier at a restaurant how much I appreciated her cheerful attitude. I thanked the nurse at my mom's assisted living facility for her dedication. I wrote a note of gratitude to someone who'd planned a huge surprise party for a friend. I was even super nice instead of angry when I needed to get a refund for an item I'd been wrongly charged for. Wherever I went—in person, on the phone, and on social media—I looked for ways to say, "You are beautiful. I see God's hand at work in your life."

Every time I shone a light on someone's inner loveliness, I felt a little better about myself. I became less focused on my world, my problems, my wrinkles, and my fat. Helping my neighbors see their value—and hopefully, believe it—made me more aware of how God sees me: one of *his purchased, special people* (see 1 Peter 2:9, AMP). I was finally able to look at myself in the mirror, grin, and say, "Hello, Beautiful!"

A few days ago, I made a bunch more magnets that said "Hello, Beautiful!" I gave one to each of the ladies in my Sunday school class. But not before I put one on my own fridge.

—Jeanette

"Happiness is like a butterfly which, when pursued, is always beyond our grasp, but, if you will sit down quietly, may alight upon you."
—**Nathaniel Hawthorne**

Beauty-full Thoughts

Do you see yourself as beautiful? Put a sticky note on your mirror or fridge that says, "Hello, Beautiful." Say those words to yourself until they feel comfortable and natural.

2

THE BEST DADDY

How great is the love the Father has lavished on us, that we
should be called children of God! And that is what we are. (1
John 3:1)

As the funeral director raised the lid on the casket that held my daddy's
body, I leaned into Mom's embrace and sobbed. Mom had brought us to
the funeral home an hour before Daddy's service so we could say goodbye
to him alone. I was ten, and my brother, Danny, was fourteen. Although
Mom was almost forty, she couldn't explain why Daddy died, nor the
alcoholism that caused his death.

Three years earlier, Mom had sat Danny and me down on the sagging
living room sofa and told us that she was divorcing Daddy. I remember
clutching the soft white blanket with pink roses Daddy had given me for
Christmas. I asked why on that day too. The only answer Mom could give
was "Daddy and I just can't get along."

Unlike me, Danny didn't ask any questions. He curled into the corner
of the sofa, tears filling his gray-green eyes that life's hard knocks eventually
turned to steel-gray. But he refused to talk about his feelings.

Several years later, Mom married Joe, another alcoholic. Although Joe
was faithful to Mom and worked hard, he made unreasonable demands,
threatened us, and called us names. I was terrified of Joe and couldn't
understand why Mom had married him. My usual cheerful personality
wilted under Joe's harsh rule, and I became withdrawn whenever he was
around.

I missed my daddy. So what if he didn't come home at night, and he
couldn't keep a job? At least he was kind, and he made us laugh. Now we
were stuck with a monster named Joe who hated us.

Seven months after Mom married Joe, we got a call that one of Daddy's friends had found him in his dingy little boardinghouse room—dead. The death certificate said cirrhosis of the liver. My sweet, funny daddy drank himself to death.

Years after Daddy's funeral, when I was old enough to understand, Mom told me about the many times she'd reconciled with Daddy after he promised to quit drinking. But he always went back to his booze once he was reassured of her love. When he got another lady pregnant and asked Mom to give him money for the abortion, Mom realized the jig was up.

Although I was glad to hear Mom's side of the story, I still questioned Daddy's death. Danny and I needed him, and he had abandoned us. I believed that Mom too had left us in the dust, choosing Joe's approval over our safety and well-being.

For many years, I blamed God for allowing these horrors to happen to our family. My self-worth suffered from the feelings of abandonment and from Joe's abuse.

In my senior year of high school, Joe became a Christian. Sitting at the kitchen table one morning, he humbled himself. "I know I've not been a very good dad to you, Jeanette. Will you please forgive me for all my orneriness over the last several years?"

With my eyes brimming, I could only nod. At that moment, I realized the power of God's love. Later that day in my bedroom, I gave my heart to Jesus as a result of Joe's night-to-day conversion.

Your life may be unlike mine. Perhaps my sorrows look tiny compared to the anguish you've suffered. I hope my story highlights one thing for you, though. God can take any situation, no matter how horrible, and turn it around for good. He is the master at taking broken lives and piecing them together. He can breathe life and beauty into any dead soul or situation.

He's the best Daddy of them all.

—Jeanette

"How beautiful a day can be when kindness touches it."
—**George Eliot**

Beauty-full Thoughts

Did you come from a broken family? Is that pain still affecting your self-worth?

❦Hello, Beautiful!

God wants to wrap his loving arms around you and help you heal.

In the lines below, write out a prayer to God, sharing your pain with him. Then write in a different colored ink what you believe he's saying to you to comfort you.

Dear God Dad always Came home yelled at me to at dinner because I wouldn't eat my peas then he would go to his room for the night as I grew older I felt like my dad was pushing me to get out of the house he always said if I want to run around naked I want to but if your here I can't Mom didn't know things that he said or did

to God I don't understand why I felt pushed to grow up sometimes if I did some kind of behavior or complaint he would tell me how I was supposed to act who I could or couldn't talk to why did he do these things

Kathleen you fathers life was dysfunctional His dad was sick and his mom he had to care for them at a young age He himself had to grow up fast he cared

for you and loved you
he did his best to help you
grow and protect-you

3

Zits, Faults, and All

"Though the mountains be shaken and the hills be removed, yet my unfailing love for you will not be shaken nor my covenant of peace be removed," says the Lord who has compassion on you. (Isaiah 54:10)

It takes courage to say, "I like myself." Especially when you've sinned, have hurt someone, or have gone off your diet for the seventh time this week.

Can you relate to any of these?

- I snap at my husband, even though I know it only makes things worse.
- I don't pray as often as I think I should, or as long.
- I get impatient with people and complain about them.
- I talk too much, listen too little, and interrupt when I'm too impatient to say something I consider more important than the person who's speaking.
- I worry about everything from how I look to what I'll do if I become a widow.
- I often leave dishes in the sink, my bed rumpled and unmade, and my furniture undusted.
- I eat too much and exercise too little.

Sometimes, I wonder if I'll ever grow up. When will I practice what I've been preaching to others for forty years? *I'm a mess.*

At a writer's conference several years ago, author Cecil Murphey prayed a simple little prayer that I later jotted down and stuck on my fridge: *Loving God, show me the truth about myself, no matter how wonderful it may be.* Aha!

God views you and me differently than we view ourselves. God sees the wonder and beauty in us, no matter how much junk is still there. Because we are hidden in Christ (Colossians 3:3), God sees us through the eyes of a Father who chooses to believe the best of his children.

That gives us courage to:
- like ourselves in spite of our boatload of flaws,
- bring our messiness to him to fix, and
- love others, no matter how imperfectly they behave.

Even before he created us, sent Jesus to die for us, and called us to himself, the Lord knew what we would be like. He's not overly concerned about our faults. He wants us to grow up, but when we aren't mature yet, his day isn't ruined like we might think.

Besides, if we were perfect, no one could stand to be around us.

I am gathering up the courage instilled in me by the God of glory and his Lamb, Jesus. I dare to say, "I like myself, zits, faults, and all." Won't you join me?

—Jeanette

"Beauty is the seasoning of virtue."
—Polish Proverb

Beauty-full Thoughts
What faults bother you the most about yourself?

That I'm a magnet for needy people
I complain too much
I talk over people
I'm always saying I'm sorry

Ask God to fix those quirks and habits and then thank him for seeing you in Christ.

Dear God I have many faults
I pray for change especially
for those I wrote down

12

Thank you for sending your
son

Now look in the mirror and say, "I like you, zits and all!"

4

A New Name

Therefore, if anyone is in Christ, the new creation has come: The old has gone, the new is here! (2 Corinthians 5:17)

Kelsey was my cute little redheaded baby girl. Jaena was only two when she was born, and having trouble with her sister's name, she pronounced Kelsey as "Cookie." When Kelsey grew out of infancy and became a toddler, her hair changed to blonde. One day, she figured she didn't belong in our family because her hair color was different from ours. She decided to run away.

"I have yellow hair. Everyone else's is brown," she announced as she walked toward the road.

Jaena leaned over the porch rail. "Cookie, come back! Come back!"

Out of love for her big sister—and because she wasn't allowed to cross the road without an adult—she came back. But to her five-year-old heart, her hair color mattered deeply. It defined who she was and where she fit into the world.

Suddenly, she was eighteen and headed to college where she transformed into a whole new person. She surprised us all and went by her first name, Johanna, instead of by her middle name, Kelsey. Now she was Jo. Kelsey had been an athlete. Jo was an artist. Kelsey had blonde hair, but Jo dyed her hair back to the red she began life with. Jo found that at college she was free to be herself, to explore new interests, and to discover hidden talents. Jo blossomed into a vibrant woman.

Sometimes we are like Jo. We need the opportunity to change, to reinvent, or to follow a new path. Maybe your children, like mine, have all flown the nest, and you're entering a whole new phase of life. Maybe you're leaving home for the first time and wonder who you are now that you have to make the decisions and pay the bills. Maybe life has sent you a curve ball, and you're facing a future you never planned on. Is this you? Or are you longing to be set free from being who others have labeled you? Too young, too old, not smart enough, not talented enough, lazy, and inadequate. Are you ready to be the woman God created you to be? Maybe you can't change your name, but how about changing your description, your title?

—**Beth**

"Comparison is the thief of joy."
—**Theodore Roosevelt**

Beauty-full Thoughts
Fill in the following sentence:
Others call me___Kathleen___, ___Kathy___
_____, and _____.
God calls me _____,
_____, and _____
_____. (You may need to sit and listen for the sweet, quiet voice of the Lord to tell you what he calls you.)

5

Jesus's Reading Material

"Neither do I condemn you," Jesus declared. "Go now and leave your life of sin." (John 8:11)

Once again, Satan—the accuser—had brought to mind a mean thing I'd said to someone years ago. As usual, the memory surfaced during a conversation I was having with Jesus. My eyes brimmed with shameful tears. My cheeks filled with fire. "Lord, I feel bad about every ornery, selfish, ugly thing I've ever done or said."

On my mind's screen flashed a picture of a fat book where I kept a record of all my sins and faults. (I was surprised there was only one volume!) The Lord of love said to me, "*You* aren't allowed to look in here. This is mine." Then he hurled that book into a huge lake, where it sank like a boulder. But before it left his hands, I saw the cover: a deep crimson liquid—his sinless blood. Yes. The cover of my book of sins was fashioned from Jesus's own blood.

Next, he showed me a slender volume, a vibrant turquoise color, which he opened and perused with a loving gaze. I knew instinctively this was the book where Jesus kept a record of all my unselfish, loving acts.

"This is the one I like to read." He gathered me into a tender embrace.

Of course, this story took place in my imagination during a time of prayer. But it fits the description of the real God/Man Jesus that we see in Scripture—the tender Good Shepherd in John 10, the nonjudgmental Rabbi in John 8, and the kind Healer in all four Gospels. Jesus would rather focus on helping us than on pointing out our faults. He's all about mercy, grace, and forgiveness.

Most of us with a low self-esteem struggle with that last sentence above. *But what about the many times Jesus came down hard on people?*

Yes, Jesus had little tolerance for those who showed off their doctor of piety degrees on the living room wall, or those who refused to believe his willingness to keep his word. But for the common person—especially the overlooked, overburdened women of his day—he offers unbounded love and understanding.

Jesus called the lady in Mark 5, who'd been weakened by twelve years of bleeding, "daughter." In the Greek, this word is an endearing term akin to darling or sweetheart. He didn't rebuke her for breaking Jewish law by being in a crowd as an unclean woman. He healed her and then commended her for her faith.

Jesus asked the Samaritan woman mentioned in John 4 for a drink. this lady had been married five times and was currently living with a man she wasn't married to. Did he berate her for her loose morals? No. He revealed himself as Messiah to her. And his kindness led her to believe in him.

The Syrophoenician woman in Matthew 15 begged for healing for her deranged daughter, and Jesus spoke a word to cast out the demon. Although he initially said no to her request, when she persisted, he changed his no to a yes. Then he complimented her for her great faith.

The only covenant these ladies had with God was based on the blood of bulls and goats. None of them were perfect. Yet, they dared to believe this teacher from Galilee would take pity on them. And Jesus gave them what they asked for. How much more will he give us—who have a covenant with God by Jesus's blood—all that we need, including a heathy view of ourselves? (See Romans 8:32)

The next time Satan opens that fat book full of accusations, let's slam it in his face and then remind him that our sins are off limits in the sea of Jesus's forgetfulness. Let's also remind ourselves God has posted a "No Fishing" sign on the shore.

—Jeanette

"Beauty seen is never lost, God's colors are all fast."
—John Greenleaf Whittier

Beauty-full Thoughts

Write your name on the blank book. As you color this picture, thank God for his forgiveness and grace.

6

QUIT PUNISHING YOURSELF

But now he has reconciled you by Christ's physical body through death to present you holy in his sight, without blemish and free from accusation. (Colossians 1:22)

At the end of my times of prayer, the Lord often whispers to my heart, "Ask for a favor." One day, I asked him to tell me what favor I could do for him. His answer shocked me. "Quit punishing yourself."

Oh, my. I didn't realize I was punishing myself. But as I pondered this strange-sounding request from the One who loves me most, I understood why God would ask this favor. I recalled how many times I had:

- Minimized a compliment someone gave me about how I looked. "This is the oldest thing in my closet. I wear it because it's comfortable"?
- Allowed the enemy to condemn me for a mistake or sin, and then wallowed in remorse and pity for days?
- Berated my intelligence or my body size, thinking of myself in terms I'd never use with anyone else?
- Tried to make up for past sins by denying myself something I liked?
- Taken responsibility for someone else's failures?

If I trust that the blood of God's Son, Jesus, is enough to erase my shame and guilt—every last ounce—why would I feel the need to punish myself? I was unconsciously telling the Lord, "I appreciate your gift, but I need to supplement it with self-abasement."

I say I believe God's grace is sufficient for my every blunder, foolish act, and wicked deed. Now I need to love myself enough to prove I believe his love. So, I made a pledge to receive God's love by inviting his grace into the areas in which I was tempted to punish myself.

- When someone complimented me, I'd simply say, "Thank you" or "I appreciate that." Period.
- When Satan came calling with waves of regret over past errors, I would quote Romans 8:1-2 and sing praises for the Lord's forgiveness. I will even tell myself, "Jeanette, I forgive you."
- When I did something ditzy or ridiculous, I'd choose to extend grace to myself, remembering that no one is exempt from mistakes.
- When I was tempted to think I needed to jump through fifteen hoops to gain God's approval, I would remind myself of the woman caught in adultery to whom Jesus said, "Neither do I condemn you; go your way and sin no more" (John 8:11).
- When a close friend, child, or other relative messed up, I'd be willing to hold them accountable and not feel responsible for their poor choices.

It's not easy—this practice of living out my belief that Jesus's sacrifice was enough for me. I have to work to believe his love for me every day. What works best for me in receiving God's unconditional love and grace?

- I say aloud, "Lord, I receive your love. I don't feel like you love me. I feel unworthy of your grace and goodness. But I choose to believe your love because you said so, and you can't lie."
- I tell God I need him to fill in my heart's holes of insecurity. It doesn't matter how they got there. I don't look for someone to blame. What I need is wholeness, and he's the one I run to for that.
- I quote as many Scriptures as I can think of about his view of me—that I'm forgiven, cleansed, made right with him, more than a conqueror, his workmanship, and much more. (Please see list of Scriptures at the end of this book for examples.)
- I accept God's grace given to me through others, whether it be in the form of a compliment, a hug, or a gift. I say, "Thank you," or "I appreciate that" as a way to reject the devil's lies that I'm unworthy of love and care.

- I refuse to beat myself up over past sins. Once I've asked God to forgive me and cleanse me, I praise him for his mercy. If they come to mind again, I remind Satan of Jesus's sacrifice for me, that his blood was enough to erase my sins forever.

As I've chosen to give up on making myself right with God by my own efforts, I've found freedom from the low self-esteem I carried most of my life. When I believe and receive his grace, I grow in beauty. It's a favor I give not only to Jesus, but also to myself.
—Jeanette

"Enjoy your life without comparing it with that of another."
—Marquis de Condorcet

Beauty-full Thoughts
Do you believe God loves you and values you? Do you catch yourself trying to make up for your sins in your own ways? List three ways you punish yourself:

_____

_____

_____

_____

Now list ways you will believe and receive his grace:

_____

_____

_____

_____

_____

7

ORNERY, UGLY, OR KIND TO YOURSELF?

Therefore, if anyone is in Christ [that is, grafted in, joined to Him by faith in Him as Savior], he is a new creature [reborn and renewed by the Holy Spirit]; the old things [the previous moral and spiritual condition] have passed away. Behold, new things have come [because spiritual awakening brings a new life]. (2 Corinthians 5:17 AMP)

We never heard the word *ornery* much until we moved from Los Angeles to the Midwest. People will say their dog is ornery, their Uncle Fred is ornery, even their newborn infant (I will *never* agree that babies qualify for the ornery label!). In another region of the country, people use the word *ugly* more often than we heard that nasty word when we lived in California.

Do you ever feel ugly? I sure do. I don't mean zits, wrinkles, or warts ugly. I mean the kind that creeps into your soul unaware and then rushes out of your mouth and mugs those around you when you and they least expect it.

- A snarky word in response to an innocent comment.
- An accusation based on your insecurities and emotions.
- A meltdown when you feel overwhelmed by too much life and too little time.
- A sharp word to a complete stranger when they offended you by their rudeness or foul language.
- A challenge to a loved one's motives.

Then afterward, you look in the mirror—whether an actual glass one, or your soul glaring back at you—and you think, *I'm ugly.*

It isn't true, you know.

Just because you and I acted from pride, insecurity, or foolishness doesn't prove that we are ugly people. We feel like failures because we didn't live up to our expectations of someone who loves with mature responses. And we're disappointed in ourselves.

But God wasn't surprised. He knew about those owies in our hearts— all the hidden pain or unspoken secrets that make us feel less than worthy. Even buried hurts we aren't aware of or won't let ourselves face. He knows. He understands. And he already planned a way to get us out of them.

It's called grace.

Grace means extending kindness and favor to someone who doesn't deserve it.

And really, none of us do. Deserve God's grace, I mean. Only because of Jesus's blood can we be called God's children. Grace has nothing to do with our perfect performance.

It has to do with our position in Christ, a position that God settled the day we said yes to Jesus and made him the Lord of our lives. Believing our position in Christ is settled will help us overcome our insecurities. Receiving his love will help us control our foolish attitudes and actions. Choosing to forgive ourselves and starting over will help us grow up emotionally.

Everyone has owies in their hearts. We discover them when we act ugly. But we don't have to believe the lie that we *are* ugly. Through God's grace, we can begin again.

It's a new day, you beautiful you! Be kind to yourself and receive God's grace.

—Jeanette

"Most folks are about as happy as they make their minds up to be."
—Abraham Lincoln

Beauty-full Thoughts
Grace: Kindness extended to someone who doesn't deserve it. List some ways you see God's grace at work in your life:

_____

_____

_____

HELLO, BEAUTIFUL!

_____

_____

_____

8

CHRISTMAS CARD KINDNESS

Each one should test their own actions. Then they can take pride in themselves alone, without comparing themselves to someone else. (Galatians 6:4)

As I flipped through the mail that snowy December afternoon, I noticed a red envelope—a Christmas card—my first of the season. In my excitement, I ripped the envelope in two and discovered a beautifully handmade card inside.

My instant reaction was, *This is gorgeous!* But I'm ashamed to admit my next thought was *Great! Not only have I not started on my own cards, but I'm also definitely not making them!*

Christmas cards are always a problem for me. I look at my December schedule each year, taking inventory of my free time and all the additional holiday projects I'd like to do. For many years, I stressed about finding random addresses, not forgetting anyone, writing the perfect newsy enclosure, and putting the cards in the mail. The task is so overwhelming in the midst of the busyness of December, it's one of the first I scratch off the list.

Yet I love receiving cards. I read them. I savor them. I display them. And I keep them. Christmas cards are one of my favorite parts of Christmas. But sending them is not something I ever get around to doing. So, I feel a lot of guilt around cards, especially the beautifully handmade ones. I have Christmas rubber stamps and cardstock waiting to be used. I miss my friends and family and want to show them my love through cards, but I rarely do.

So, for a few minutes that afternoon, I held my friend's card and fell into the comparison trap. Why can't I make time for this? Why, when I do find time, are my cards store bought? *I'm such a bad friend. I should be like her.*

Suddenly, the Spirit whispered in my ear, *Let her enjoy her hobby. Be thankful that she thought of you, that she had fun celebrating Christmas the way she wanted. Celebrate this Christmas and your friend by being thankful, not guilty or jealous of her time and her talent. How do you suppose she would feel if she knew what you were thinking right now? She would be dismayed, right? Do you really want her to be sad because she spent time making this for you?*

Then and there, I decided to place her card in the middle of the Christmas decorations as a reminder to be thankful for my friend.

Do you ever react with jealousy or guilt when someone does a kindness for you? Ask God to help you be grateful for being in someone's thoughts and for being loved.

—Beth

"In all ranks of life the human heart yearns for the beautiful; and the beautiful things that God makes are his gifts to all alike."

—Harriet Beecher Stowe

Beauty-full Thoughts

Find some pictures of friends or a gift from a friend. Put their picture somewhere that will remind you to thank God for them.

9

THE APOLOGY

Love your neighbor as yourself. (Mark 12: 31 NASB)

"Oops, my report printed in lavender again." My co-worker, Allen, smiled as he removed the bright paper and reloaded with white.

I could feel the heat filling my face. "Oh, I'm sorry. I forgot again." I wondered how long it would take me to remember to replace my colored paper with white in the copier Allen and I shared. After all, I'd been at this job eight months. What was my problem?

"That's okay," said Allen. "I'll make another copy."

I sighed in relief and went back to work.

During my break, I told Allen how relieved I felt when he told me not to worry regarding my purple paper bungle. "That's the first time since I started here that you've told me you forgave me over a mistake I apologized for. All the other times, you were silent. I thought maybe you were disgusted with me."

Allen smiled. "Well, I figured your mistakes are not that big a deal. If you stole my stash of dark chocolate I keep under my desk, you'd definitely need to ask forgiveness. But with minor annoyances like lavender paper, you just fix it and move along."

I stared at him in astonishment. "Is that how it was in your house growing up? Most of us were raised with guilt and shame."

"In our family, if you made a mistake, you simply said, 'Sorry,' and then everyone went ahead with their lives. No need to ask forgiveness or make a big deal."

I wondered if he realized how rare his family was, how full of grace. To have your parents and siblings simply go on living after you made a mistake, especially one that inconvenienced someone, was unheard of in our family.

No wonder it was difficult for me to believe that when I failed or sinned, the Father forgave me immediately and then forgot it. No wonder I blamed myself for everything from a rained-out picnic (I forgot to pray for sunshine) to my daughter's first C grade (I didn't quiz her enough).

I realized I needed to extend the same grace to myself that Allen had practiced in his life. But how to overcome decades of taking too much responsibility for minor blunders, for allowing perfectionism to steal my joy?

I began with baby steps.

If my husband accidentally kicked a bowl of cat food across the kitchen, I simply cleaned it up or asked him if he needed help cleaning. If someone at my church got mad at me for misspelling their name in a newspaper article I authored, I said, "I apologize" once then didn't allow myself to re-apologize three more times in hopes she wouldn't hold a grudge. If I left lavender paper in the copier, I said "Oops! Let me replace that for you, and I'll bring you the copy when it's done."

It's not easy. Sometimes I feel like I'm being prideful and flippant. But it's more fun than living under the dark cloud of condemnation, of always feeling the need to take the blame for minor mistakes.

I'm doing what Jesus taught: loving myself. It feels like flying out of a cage I'd been imprisoned in all my life. Wanna try it? Baby steps will get you there.

—Jeanette

"Dare to be what you are and learn to resign with a good grace all that you are not and to believe in your own individuality."

—Henri-Frederic Amiel

Beauty-full Thoughts

Are there things in your life you aren't forgiving yourself for?

_____

_____

_____

_____

Can you ask God to help you have a forgiving heart?

_____

_____

_____

_____

What baby steps will you take to help yourself receive God's forgiveness and move on?

_____

_____

_____

_____

_____

_____

_____

10

Have Some Dirt, Please

Therefore, if you have any encouragement from being united with Christ, if any comfort from his love, if any common sharing in the Spirit, if any tenderness and compassion, then make my joy complete by being like-minded, having the same love, being one in spirit and of one mind. (Philippians 2:1-2)

I swiped my finger beneath the swag of silk daisies on Gloria's windowsill and sighed in bliss. *Oh goody, dirt. She is human after all.*

Every other time we'd visited Gloria and Lee, their home sparkled. Not a thread out of place or a crumb unswept. And I was jealous.

Although I continually joked about my lack of housekeeping genes, I secretly wished I were more conscientious and tidier. When I found someone who enjoyed cleaning house and decorating, I had this love/hate thing going on.

I loved being around them, because they had all the discipline and enthusiasm for neatness that I didn't. But I hated being around them because they reminded me of my lack of domestic leanings. I felt inferior.

So, finding dust in Gloria's house was the happy surprise I needed to chase the torment away. But only for a minute. After my initial elation, I was a mite ashamed of my immature attitude toward these dear friends. Instead of rejoicing when I found a little grime, shouldn't I be happy for their talent to keep an orderly, clean home?

Then I realized why we like to discover dust in other's homes and lives. No one wants to feel alone in his or her weaknesses. If we find someone with the same faults as ours or worse, that revelation comforts us and releases us from self-condemnation.

This explains why some people love to find flaws in others and spread nasty secrets about them, whether true or not. And why millions buy idiotic magazines with squalid stories about famous people. We crave dirt on others' windowsills to make our own muck seem less harmful. *Wow, I may have a lot of shortcomings, but at least I don't* _____.

The problem with this kind of attitude? We never feel better about ourselves for more than a few seconds. Deep inside our hearts where Jesus lives, we realize everyone is broken, but in different places. Only God's love and grace can make us whole. Once we embrace that truth and turn to him for healing, we'll not only extend mercy to ourselves for our shortcomings, but we'll also view others' dirt in a new way. We'll realize we're only responsible for our own messes, not anyone else's. I don't know about you, but I have too many dust bunnies in my soul to go pointing out the smudges in yours.

Next time I visit Gloria and Lee, I'll be looking for fellowship, not grime. And if you come to my house, please don't even go near the windowsills!

—Jeanette

"Every year of my life I grow more convinced that it is wisest and best to fix our attention on the beautiful and the good, and dwell as little as possible on the evil and the false."

—Richard Cecil

Beauty-full Thoughts
How are you tempted to find the dirt in others' lives?

_____

_____

_____

_____

Next time you find yourself searching for grime on someone else's soul, how will you reinforce your belief in God's love and grace for yourself?

_____

_____

_____

_____

11

PERFUME-MANIA

Dear friend, you are faithful in what you are doing for the brothers and sisters, even though they are strangers to you. (3 John 1:5)

When a friend at work sent an email around that her parents' home had burned to the ground, I put together a box with some extra towels from the linen closet, a few kitchen utensils, and some mixing bowls. Then a little thought bubbled up from my heart. Why don't I give Mrs. Engle some of my perfume? I had more than enough, and she'd probably enjoy something personal, rather than only this practical stuff.

I recognized that still, small voice, and reached for a bottle of perfume I rarely used. *Hey, Jeanette, don't give her a bottle you never wear that you're getting rid of. Give her one of your favorites.*

Oh, dear! I had recently purchased an angelic scent I'd fallen in love with. Could God really mean for me to give that to a total stranger, someone I never met? Without allowing myself time to change my mind, I tucked the precious perfume into the box with the other items.

The following week, my coworker told me how thrilled her mom was with the perfume, delighted that someone had thought to give her a delicate gift among all the practical household items. I was happy I had obeyed that sweet, inner prompting of the Lord.

But that's not the end of the story. A few days later, another friend gave me a bottle of perfume she'd purchased and wasn't too fond of. You guessed it—the identical scent I gave away, only a bigger bottle! I thanked her and rejoiced that God had set me up for a blessing.

Thus, began a season of *Perfume-mania Harvest*. People have given me perfume they were tired of. I've received perfume as gifts. And my husband has found my favorite scents at yard sales for next to nothing. All I did was obey the Lord by giving away one small item I was fond of, and he's been overwhelming me with perfume ever since.

I'm sometimes convicted of how I pamper my body, how I expect to have seven or eight different perfumes, hand lotions, and hair products to make myself feel and look beautiful. I'm privileged indeed.

God's priorities are opposite from what we humans value. He places significance on inner loveliness. Want to know what qualities impress him? Things like sharing, helping, and praying for others. We might look in the mirror and see gray hairs and wrinkles. But if we have a heart to obey the Lord and love others, God sees a perfect countenance, one free of selfishness and pride.

As he dances in joy over our pure heart, he says, *Hello, Beautiful! I am so proud of you.*

I may not be as rich and gorgeous as I'd like to be. But I have enough to share with others. That makes my Father and me very happy.

—Jeanette

"Always be a little kinder than necessary."
—James M. Barrie

Beauty-full Thoughts

How is your heart today? Are you concentrating on your outer beauty or your inner beauty? Meditate for a few moments on the fruit of the Spirit.

The fruits of the Spirit are (Galatians 5:22-23)	How can God use me to show this fruit?
Love	
Joy	

The fruits of the Spirit are (Galatians 5:22-23)	How can God use me to show this fruit?
Peace	
Patience	
Kindness	
Goodness	
Faithfulness	
Gentleness	
Self-control	

12

Cooking Up Confidence

> Dear friends, do not believe every spirit, but test the spirits to see whether they are from God, because many false prophets have gone out into the world. (1 John 4:1)

Five of us, including a couple old friends and a few new acquaintances, sat around the wooden farmhouse table. We spent the afternoon getting to know each other better through a meandering flow of subjects punctuated with moments of laughter. As the conversation transitioned from exercise to food preferences, my friend Lynn offered to make dinner the next day for us all.

Everyone agreed. "That would be great!"

"Thanks!"

"Sure."

"I'd love it.'

"That's kind of you."

I knew her meal would be great because I'd enjoyed many of her prepared dishes before. She loved to cook and was a natural, one of those people who never needed a recipe. Instead, she *created* dishes—unlike me, who followed recipes with precise measurements.

Without thinking, I pointed at Lynn and said, "She hates my cooking."

"It's fine if you like eating cardboard," she responded.

I jabbed her playfully in the ribs and laughed, hoping to hide my embarrassment and shame. This wasn't the first time she'd criticized my food with the cardboard comment. I thought of many of my attempts at tasty meals that Lynn had critiqued through the years.

Sam told her to be nice to me. Everyone laughed. The conversation moved on with no one noticing my discomfort. But her words settled into my heart with the heaviness of stones.

I sat there thinking and realized I'd been carrying her criticism around my neck like a label. I'd done that for years. My family became my sounding board as I quizzed them with questions of whether my food tasted good. Soon, my self-criticism convinced me to stop serving in a meal ministry to new moms. In my opinion, my dishes simply weren't tasty enough. Since my daughter enjoyed cooking and was good at it, I talked her into fixing supper often.

"Better than me," had become my label. "Everyone is better than me. I'm not a good cook. I should let others do it."

Recently, my daughter, now living on her own, asked me for my recipes. A friend told me she loved when I made food for her. Someone else complimented a dish I made that Lynn had criticized earlier at the same potluck. Had I been believing a lie? I thought about the meals I made at home for my family and realized I loved to cook and loved to eat what I prepared. I don't know why Lynn decided to criticize my cooking, but I understand now that she wasn't speaking truth into my life.

I could have blessed so many more new moms through my meals if I hadn't quit because of my insecurities. I could have found joy, not anxiety, in preparing meals for friends and family. I could have been improving my skills instead of believing that I could never be a good cook. But by accepting a lie as the truth, I was hindered from doing something I love and am actually quite good at.

I wonder how much of our self-doubt is influenced by the lies of others. How much time do we waste believing cruel comments, taking them as truth? How could God be using us if we stopped believing those lies?

—Beth

"Hold up your head! You were not made for failure, you were made for victory. Go forward with a joyful confidence."
—George Eliot

Beauty-full Thoughts

Have you ever been ridiculed in front of others? How did you hide your embarrassment? What ways can you test to see if those cruel words are lies?

_____

_____

HELLO, BEAUTIFUL!

_____

_____

_____

_____

_____

13

All Gods on This Shelf

Whoever believes in me, as Scripture has said, rivers of living water will flow from within them. (John 7:38)

When Kevin was between ministries for ten years, he worked at a collection agency in the Chinatown area of LA. He'd often use part of his lunch hour to browse the interesting shops full of lacquered jewelry boxes, rice candies, and fans painted in bright watercolors—some large enough to hang on a wall.

One night at dinner, he told me what he'd seen that day in a shop. "A bright hand-lettered sign under a shelf full of plastic idols caught my eye," he said. "When I bent to read the sign, it said 'All gods on this shelf half price.'"

I was tempted to make fun of those who worship gods that machines or hands have made until I realized the types of items I often make into idols.

My top idol is shopping. I'll come out of a coma for a neighborhood yard sale or a fifty-percent-off coupon at my favorite clothing store. I don't think God is opposed to my penchant for buying, especially gifts for others. Unless I go into debt to buy them. Then my spending becomes a way to make myself feel significant. I use shopping as a drug that overcomes my feelings of inferiority. I've become a slave to that emotional charge (pun intended) I get when I buy, buy, buy.

My next favorite idol is food. During a recent illness when I was severely limited as to food choices, I realized how important food is to me. Too important. I whined and cried, feeling deprived and underprivileged (I would have made a great Israelite, complaining about the tasteless manna).

When I finally recovered after one of the longest months of my life, I prayed about this idol. "Lord, I can see that food is too important to me. I use it as a way to not only feed my belly but to entertain my tongue." Even though God knows everything about me, I was still embarrassed to admit that this kind of idolatry was a form of worshipping myself, because I feel less than beautiful.

Yes, that's the root of my idolatry. Whether I spend, eat, or talk too much to gain attention, I use these to make me feel better about myself instead of crying out to God for encouragement.

I love this about God: he didn't get angry with me when I admitted I was using shopping and food as idols. He forgave me like he said he would in 1 John 1:9, then gave me a few ideas about living within my means and curbing my appetite. Most importantly, he reassured me of his deep, eternal love via his Word, the Bible, and the kindness of others. All I had to do was ask for his help.

I can't fill up my emotional gas tank by spending, slurping, or showing off. Only God's love can satisfy my craving for significance. And there's nothing cheap about that.

—Jeanette

"If you see any beauty in Christ, and say, 'I desire to have that,' God will work it in you."

—G.V. Wigram

Beauty-full Thoughts

What ways might you sometimes try to make yourself feel worthy of love? Have any of those methods become idols?

_____

_____

_____

_____

_____

_____

If so, please don't condemn yourself. Simply ask God to help you replace the counterfeits with his genuine, unconditional love.

_____

_____

_____

_____

14

TRADE A TROUBLE

Be content with what you have. (Hebrews 13:5)

While recently attending my own pity party, I played the game "Trade My Troubles for Yours." In my game, I envisioned a huge vending machine brimming with better issues than my own. My problems were messy. A quick temper that reflects my fire-colored hair. Boundary issues in the workplace. An aging parent to care for. But I knew dozens of people who had lesser problems I'd love to try out for a day or a lifetime. Or so I thought.

I'd tuck my intolerable troubles into the slot. Then I'd punch the number of the problem I was willing to bear.

My first choice was #45: Famous. I could put up with that. The phone ringing every hour with requests to appear on interview programs, endorsing the newest kitchen gadgets, my photo on magazine covers.

As the card with the printed problem exits the machine, I grab it with gusto and read, "When you eat in a restaurant, you must ask for a secluded table where no one can see you. Otherwise, you'll be signing autographs in between bites. Everywhere you go people will hound you, asking how you achieved success and telling you their woeful stories." *Well, maybe that one's not much fun after all.* I toss that card in the trash.

I punch another button that looks more promising, #98: Gorgeous body and hair. That wouldn't be all that tough. I'd be invited to everyone's parties, and handsome waiters would fawn over me.

This card says, "Other women don't like to be around you because your stunning good looks intimidate them. Some people want to be your friend only because you're attractive. You have few genuine friends, so you're often lonely." *Scrap that one.*

What else might suit me better than my current predicaments? *Aha, here's a dandy!* I punch #102: Genius. That's no problem.

Then I read, "You get impatient with everyone who isn't as smart as you are. They're all either jealous of you because you're a genius, or they don't know how to talk to you. So, you have no friends."

I sigh. I'm only kidding myself to think that everyone's difficulties are less troublesome than mine are.

Then I recall the hundreds of times the Lord sent the perfect people, songs, books, and words of Scripture to encourage me in my moments of despair. Although I don't believe he ordained my problems, he knew which ones to allow.

Before he shaped the world and named the stars, he knew what type of personality I'd have, who my parents would be, and what I could endure without falling apart.

The same is true for us all.

God's love is bigger than our issues. His grace is deeper than our despair. When we look to him, instead of playing "Trade a Trouble," we'll rest in the assurance that as he's given us strength in the past to walk through a valley, he'll continue to share his abundant grace with us in the future. He's never shocked by our messiest maladies, because he's already blueprinted the solutions.

I decide to end the pity party by reaching into the machine and retrieving my own problems, the only ones God has given me the grace to manage and the holiness to overcome.

These are *my* problems. "Welcome back!"

—Jeanette

"To forget oneself is to be happy."
—Robert Louis Stevenson

Beauty-full Thoughts

Do you like your personality? Is there some characteristic you think you'd like to exchange? Name that characteristic:

_____

_____

_____

_____

Now think about how your life would be with the opposite characteristic. Would you still want to change? Ask God for help being contented with how he created you.

_____

_____

_____

_____

_____

15

A Few of My Favorite Things

Therefore the LORD waits [expectantly] and longs to be gracious
to you,
And therefore He waits on high to have compassion on you.
For the LORD is a God of justice;
Blessed (happy, fortunate) are all those who long for Him [since
He will never fail them] (Isaiah 30:18, AMP)

Do you remember the Julie Andrew's song, "My Favorite Things," from *The Sound of Music?* Each of us has our own list of things we think about to cheer ourselves up when we are sad, lonely, or discouraged. Mine would include:

- Giggling babies and children
- Colors, especially friendly ones like orange, turquoise, and chartreuse
- Ice cream, apricots, and rainbow trout
- Soil under my fingernails and grass stains on my knees while gardening
- Laughing 'til my sides ache
- Sliding across the kitchen floor in my stockinged feet
- Words, especially fun-to-say words like *capricious* and *obtuse*

Recently, I was thinking of what my favorite things are about living in a rural area of the country. These are just a few of the many:

- Cardinals on the wing in a snowy meadow
- The still, holy hush of dawn
- God's paintbrush dripping mauve and peach onto a sunset sky

- A garden bursting at its seams
- Harvested grain auguring into a truck bed
- People who care enough to ask and patient enough to listen

Then there's God. If I listed all my favorite things about him, I would never be finished, but I have some I especially appreciate:

- He believes in us, whether we believe in him or not.
- We can be ourselves with him. He's never shocked by our foolishness or failures.
- He has endless methods up his sleeves for solving horrible problems.
- He isn't only able to help, heal and, prosper us. He actually wants to.
- He's on our side when we feel like the whole world is against us.
- He knows what we're like deep inside, and he still likes us. Wow!

And, did you know God himself has a list of favorite things? What do you imagine is on it? Only one item:

You!

I know, I feel challenged to believe that too, especially on a day when I've lost my temper because of a disappointment, or when the sky fills with gray clouds and SAD—seasonal affective disorder—shows up *again,* or the hormone demons are having a party in my soul, or ...

All of the above may be facts that try to hinder me from believing I'm one of God's favorite kids. They may even tempt me to doubt if he wants to keep me in the family album. But they are not truths which come from his Word, and which never change with my moods or the seasons. A few of those truths that help me love—even like—myself in spite of myself are:

- God is always thinking about me (Psalm 139:17-18).
- The Lord wants, even longs, to bless and favor me (Isaiah 30:18).
- God causes everything to work out for my good (Romans 8:28).
- I am loved by God and called to be a saint (Romans 1:7).
- Jesus does not condemn me. He prays for me (Romans 8:34).
- The minute I confess my sins, God forgives me and cleanses me (1 John 1:9).

- Jesus in me is greater than all the forces of evil around me (1 John 4:4).

These same truths apply to you if you belong to Jesus Christ. On our worst day, God doesn't change his mind about our position in his family or his love for us. He is committed to us as his dearly loved children, the sheep of his fold, and his precious, beautiful creations.

We all are his favorites.

—Jeanette

"Never lose an opportunity of seeing anything that is beautiful; for beauty is God's handwriting—a wayside sacrament; welcome it in every fair face, every fair sky, every fair flower, and thank him for it."

—Charles Kingsley

Beauty-full Thoughts

What are some of your favorite things?

_____

_____

_____

_____

_____

Which of the truths listed in the Scriptures above do you need to be reminded of today?

_____

_____

_____

_____

16

COURAGE THROUGH FAILURE

*Let us not become weary in doing good, for at the proper time
we will reap a harvest if we do not give up. (Galatians 6:9)*

When Jaena's name popped up on my caller ID, I quickly hit answer.
"Guess what, Mom. I made a traveling music team this semester!"

We were both equally shocked and excited. Making a team had been a
long-sought-after and hard-earned achievement for her. She'd persisted in
trying out every school year and was turned down every time until now,
her final year.

My mom heart ached each time I watched Jaena wrestle with
disappointment. Eventually, she began to doubt her abilities. But at the
same time, I was proud to watch her never give up. That phone call was one
of the most precious calls I've ever received.

Why do we so easily give up when rejected and tell ourselves we aren't
good enough when sometimes the rejection isn't about our abilities but
about timing or the particular need of the one making the choice? It's
important to learn the difference between rejection based on merit and
rejection based on outside forces. Most times, successful people aren't
naturally better than others. Instead, they try again and again until they're
the ones chosen. They know that every attempt makes them a little bit
better than they were before.

Each time my daughter tried out for a new team, she learned more about
what was needed to be successful, and she improved in those areas between
tryouts until she was qualified for the job. Jaena grew more confident as she
learned what those hiring wanted and needed and as she began to see the
difference between a choice based on talent and one based on need.

This plays out in life all the time. Two singers may be equal in talent,
but the solo is written for a soprano. The long-distance runner will beat the

sprinter in a two-mile race. You and I may both be great cooks, but your lasagna may taste better than mine and my cookies better than yours. One artist is able to paint beautifully with watercolors while another excels at oils.

Is there something in your life that has been a source of rejection? Did you quit? Should you consider persisting and discovering how to improve with each rejection?

—Beth

"Failure is only postponed success as long as courage 'coaches' ambition. The habit of persistence is the habit of victory."

—Herbert Kaufman

Beauty-full Thoughts

Pray and journal about that area in your life where you feel rejection.

_____

_____

_____

_____

_____

_____

Is that area important enough to you to keep trying? List some ways you can become better at the skills needed.

_____

_____

_____

_____

_____

_____

_____

Pick one to work on this week.

_____

17

Dream a Big Dream with Me

"For I know the plans I have for you," declares the Lord, "plans to prosper you and not to harm you, plans to give you hope and a future." (Jeremiah 29:11)

When I was a little girl, I dreamed of marrying a wealthy man and owning a mansion with a swimming pool. As a teenager, I dreamed of writing books and traveling the world to sing opera in lavish costumes.

Most people think only one of my dreams came true—I am an author. But I would argue about the definition of the word *wealthy* in relation to my husband. True, we don't own a mansion with a swimming pool. But he is a faithful, godly man who cares for me more than his own life, and you can't trade that for all the stuff in the world. So, I contend that two of my three biggest dreams are now reality.

I let go of the other one after I realized I love writing and being a wife more than starving myself to fit into opera costumes and practicing vocal scales four hours a day. Also, because I don't like opera music!

Other dreams—traveling the world, winning a million people into God's family, owning a home in the country—have taken shape in recent years. I know, I know. They're enormous dreams that need an enormous God to make them happen. That's okay. My God is bigger than my doubts.

I read recently that people who write down their dreams earn nine times as much over their lifetime as those who don't. Wow! That made me skedaddle to find a pad and pen!

Those of us with low self-esteem may find it difficult to dream. *Who am I kidding? I can barely get dressed and stay in my right mind every day. Dreaming big, even little dreams, won't get me out of the mess I'm in.*

Let me tweak that thinking a bit.

You were created in God's image. God is a dreamer. He dreamed of the cosmos before he spoke it into being. He dreamed of a plan whereby his children who'd lost their way in the darkness of the world could become friends with him again. And he continues to dream of the abundant life he wants to give all his kids (Jesus's words in John 10:10 and the Father's promise in Jeremiah 29:11).

Instead of trying to muster a bit of faith on your own, will you let God dream through you? Will you dare to ask him to pour some of his outrageous hopes and plans and goals into your heart? His dreams for you are high and wide and deep. He's not a wimpy, wish-upon-a-star god. He has all the power in the universe at his disposal, to make his dreams reality in your life. Will you dare to ask him to fill your soul with desires that shock even you? Will you allow yourself to dream big—bigger than you ever have before?

What would you like to do, to be, to achieve, to create? What dream is so much bigger than you are that you recognize it as a God-thing when that dream comes true? Don't settle for wishing on a star when you can have the Milky Way. If you're a child of Almighty God, dare to dream with him.

Because the thing about dreams is that they come true only if you dream them. And if you need a pen and paper, I have extra to share.

—Jeanette

"The future belongs to those who believe in the beauty of their dreams."
—Eleanor Roosevelt

Beauty-full Thoughts
List your dreams.

_____

_____

_____

_____

_____

_____

Commit them to God, and then watch what he will do!

_____

_____

_____

_____

18

God Likes Farmers

It is because of the LORD's lovingkindnesses that we are not consumed, because His [tender] compassions never fail. They are new every morning; great and beyond measure is Your faithfulness. (Lamentations 3: 22-23 AMP)

God likes farmers. How do I know? Because Jesus, who was God in a body, talked a great deal about them and repeatedly used them in his teaching. He told stories about planting in different kinds of soil (Matthew 13:3-23), enemies sowing weeds in your field (Matthew 13:24-30), and small seeds becoming huge plants (Matthew 13:32). He even compared good seeds to sons of the kingdom and weeds to the sons of the devil (Matthew 13:37-43).

When our son Ron was three years old, he toted a sack of grass clippings into the living room.

"What are you doing, Ron? Please don't get grass all over the carpet."

"But Mommy, this is in case Daddy decides to quit being a preacher and becomes a farmer. He'll need something to feed the cows!"

That idea lasted a big ten seconds. Kevin burst Ron's bubble by telling him God had called him to tend believers, not bovines.

In a sense, Kevin is a farmer. He stands in the pulpit twice every Sunday, planting God's Word in his field of our hearts. He plants the Word again when he teaches a Bible school lesson or writes a song. When he visits and prays for those who are home or hospital-bound, he is planting seeds of kindness and comfort. So, Ron got his wish after all but in a different way than he planned.

You and I are farmers too. Every day we plant seeds, and every day we reap the harvest of what we planted yesterday, last week, and ten years ago.

We cannot get away from this truth: we reap whatever we sow (Galatians 6:7). We choose our crop by our words, our attitudes, even our thoughts. All these things are seeds. The events of our lives result from planting and reaping, sowing and harvesting, day after day.

Not excited about that thought? Perhaps you, like me, have sown a lot of rotten seed over the years. Sometimes we bumbled, not knowing we were planting heartache and pain. Other times we were just plain rebellious. We knew God wanted us to keep our negative thoughts to ourselves or to control some unhealthy appetite, but we stubbornly forged ahead anyway. Then we found our fellowship with the Lord and others choked by nasty weeds. Praying became a chore. Reading God's Word went from delight to duty.

Before you despair, keep reading. God's plan is full of hope.

Unlike natural planting and harvest time, the Father lets us begin new every day. His mercy and compassion are like a fresh, sun-drenched morning. When we ask his forgiveness and turn our back on sin, he allows us to start over. Then he empowers us with his gracious Holy Spirit to sow good, healthy seed in our field and in the fields of those around us.

Even if we spill grass clippings all over the room, he's there to help us clean up the mess.

—Jeanette

"The flower of youth never appears more beautiful than when it bends toward the sun of righteousness."
—Matthew Henry

Beauty-full Thoughts
How is God using you to plant seeds and water lives?

_____

_____

_____

_____

_____

_____

Is he showing you new ways he wants to use you? List a few here.

_____

_____

_____

_____

19

CHATTERBOX OR CHEERLEADER

Yet grace [God's undeserved favor] was given to each one of us [not indiscriminately, but in different ways] in proportion to the measure of Christ's [rich and abundant] gift. (Ephesians 4:7 AMP)

When I was a child, my mom often called me a chatterbox. She would ask, "Who wound you up?" as if I were a toy monkey. Others teased me for my penchant for talking. In my narrow world, adults could talk as much as they liked, and no one rebuked them. But children were considered rude if they chattered.

So, I grew up with the belief that talking a lot was a character flaw. When you believe something about yourself, whether it's true or not, your belief colors your feelings. I became ashamed of my gift of gab. I prayed to listen more than I talked. I berated myself when I kept Kevin waiting after church while I visited with a friend—or ten.

As an adult, however, I discovered my gift—communication. Now we know where the source of my desire to talk, sing, teach, and write all those words originated: from the giver of all good gifts (See James 1:17). I've found there's a difference between chattering to fill up empty space and communicating.

When I say or write something that lifts another out of a deep well of despair or tweaks erroneous thinking about the Father, I'm communicating his heart of love and grace. When I pray with someone to receive physical or emotional healing, I'm cooperating with the Great Physician to bring his will to earth. When I sing a song of comfort, I'm helping Jesus open the door to someone's broken heart.

I often ask the Lord to keep a watch at the door of my mouth so I don't chatter. I want my words to count for eternity. To lift up, build, and reveal his goodness and wisdom. To nourish a soul or a million souls. To pass on his heart that spills over with love for you. Even to make you laugh so you'll be healthier. This is communicating my Lord to you. And it's a gift, not a curse.

These days I choose to embrace my gift of words. I'm more than a chatterbox. I'm a cheerleader for God.

You have a gift too. Perhaps you love to write fantasy stories, send greeting cards to lonely people, knit mittens and hats, create yummy recipes, or sketch animals. Because of my childhood experience, I can imagine that in your growing up years someone tried to make you feel ashamed of your gift. A person you admired teased you or twisted the truth to make you think your gift was a character flaw. Or at the very least, unimportant.

I'd like to challenge you to let Jesus shine the light of his love on your gifts. To show you how important they are to him and to others. He gave them to you. He wants you to use them, even revel in them, and feel his pleasure as you share them with others. Then watch the beauty inside you blossom forth to bless every heart around you, including your own.

—Jeanette

"Loving God, show me the truth about myself—no matter how wonderful it may be."[1]
—Cecil Murphey

Beauty-full Thoughts
Have you been teased into believing your gift is a curse? How can that gift be redeemed into something positive?

_____

_____

_____

_____

_____

_____

---

1   Cecil Murphy, in a speech given at the Southern Christian Writer's Conference, Tuscaloosa, AL, June 2016. Used by permission.

Dare to ask God the wonderful ways in which he sees you!

_____

_____

_____

_____

_____

20

CREATED WITH A PURPOSE

Praise God in his sanctuary; praise him in his mighty heavens.
Praise him for his acts of power; praise him for his surpassing greatness.
Praise him with the harp and lyre, praise him with timbrel and dancing,
Praise him with the clash of cymbals, praise him with resounding cymbals.
Let everything that has breath praise the Lord. Praise the Lord. (Psalm 150:1-6)

Pam stood, placed her clarinet to her lips, and improvised a tune, tapping her foot to keep the beat. Then she closed her eyes and swayed with the rhythm. She was as much fun for me to watch as she was to listen to. When she finished and sat back down, her face was lit with a huge grin. It was obvious she'd been living in the music. In those moments, she was completely unaware of the audience sitting a few feet in front of her. Pam came alive in her passion for music. While she played, she was doing the thing she was created to do. And everyone in the room was given a special gift by being able to witness it.

Isn't it amazing that God's purpose for some people is to praise him through musical instruments? Pam was fulfilling God's purpose in her life that day. *Four thousand are to be gatekeepers and four thousand are to praise the Lord with the musical instruments I have provided for that purpose* (1 Chronicles 23:5).

We are all created to praise God and bring him glory. How do we do that? I believe when we use the talents God gave us, we honor and glorify God. When we realize what we're created to do, we come alive. Like Pam, we can lose track of time and our surroundings. We find energy and strength in passionately serving, teaching, creating, and other such endeavors.

Unfortunately, many of us don't recognize what our talent is, or we don't give ourselves permission to do what comes naturally. We lie to ourselves and think it's too easy or too small and inconsequential to be worthwhile to God.

I've been guilty of thinking that God cares only about the big, the difficult, or the visible service. But I worshiped God as I watched Pam lose herself in sharing the talent God gave her. If we aren't careful, we might never feel the same joy she felt in those minutes. And I don't believe that's God's wish for us.

Mediate on 1 Chronicles 23:5. Then ask God to reveal to you what he created you to do.

Is it singing? Sing out loud.

Do you love to write notes of encouragement? Write those notes with confidence.

Can you bake? Bake a cake with a song in your heart.

Does it fill you with joy to play with children? Play till you drop.

Do babies love for you to cuddle them? Cuddle away.

Is it making others laugh? Be funny with abandon.

How about teaching? Then teach and be grateful for your knowledge.

Ask God to show you how he wants to use you today for his glory. Then take that first brave step toward glorifying your Creator.

—Beth

"The best, most beautiful, and most perfect way that we have of expressing a sweet concord of mind to each other is by music."
—Jonathan Edwards

Beauty-full Thoughts

Consider what your talent or talents might be, what you were created to do. Write it/them down.

_____

_____

_____

_____

_____

_____

How might you cultivate an unused talent?

_____

_____

_____

_____

Now write one way you'll use one of those talents to glorify God *today*.

_____

_____

21

Mighty Peace

And the peace of God, which transcends all understanding, will guard your hearts and your minds in Christ Jesus. (Philippians 4:7)

Several years ago, I wrote a song for a dear friend who was going through a terrible time. I didn't have the words to say that would ease her pain or banish her fears. But somehow, when I sang the message, the words reached into her heart in a way no simple speaking could do. This is the song I wrote and later sang to her many times during her fiery trial:

Your mighty peace
Will comfort me
When all around the storms besiege.
I will hide
Beneath your wing
And rest my soul
In your mighty peace.
Though Satan lie
And tempt me sore,
Within your Word I am secure.
I will stand
Forevermore.
Your mighty peace
Will win each war.

When Kevin heard the song, he said, "Isn't that kind of contradictory? I never thought of God's peace being mighty. It's calm and soothing."

And being the submissive wife that I am, I said, "You're right, dear" and quickly changed the words.

Absolutely not! I left the song just as it was. Because to me, when you're fighting a battle with the devil, whether he attacks you with lack of confidence, poor health, challenges in your finances, or a messed-up relationship, God's peace in the midst of all that turmoil is the most powerful weapon there is.

When Satan throws his best problems and worst lies at you, trying to steal your peace with worry, you can go to God's Word and claim his promises. Then simply rest in him and refuse to panic or worry. This counter-attack forces the devil to retreat. The accuser whispers, "No one cares about you."

But you open your Bible to Isaiah 49:15-16 and say, "Shut up, devil! Even if my mother forgets me, God will never forget me. He's carved me on the palm of his hand!"

He tries again with, "You're stupid."

And you counter that lie with a truth from 1 Corinthians 2:16. "I have the mind of Christ. Get behind me, Satan!" You focus your mind and your words and on the answer rather than the problem. You speak to your mountain of doubt, insecurity, and fear (Mark 11:22-24). That will cause the peace to come and the devil to run.

We may not understand how the words in a book called the Bible can be so alive that they bring peace to our troubled souls, but that's okay. We don't need to understand God's Word for it to work. The apostle Paul wrote that God's peace *transcends all understanding* (Philippians 4:7). It jumps the track of our reasoning and goes straight to the heart where it can do the most good.

His peace is mighty. And it's available to you. Open the Book and dig in.

—Jeanette

"Everything that is made beautiful and fair and lovely, is made for the eye of one who sees."
—Rumi

Beauty-full Thoughts
How do you need God's peace in the war you are fighting right now?

Spend some time thanking him for his peace in your situation.

Look up a verse or passage about God's peace and write out the words below.

22

DROPPING THE BELL

If I should say, "My foot has slipped," Your lovingkindness, O LORD, WILL HOLD ME UP. WHEN MY ANXIOUS THOUGHTS MULTIPLY WITHIN ME, YOUR CONSOLATIONS DELIGHT MY SOUL. (Psalm 94:18-19 NASB)

This was our first time to ring the Salvation Army bell on one of the coldest weekends of the year in our Midwestern town. I bundled up in several layers, including mittens, which I'd heard keep hands warmer than gloves. My breath came out like spurts of warm fog every time I said, "Merry Christmas" to the shoppers who braved icy roads and freezing air.

My musically talented husband, Kevin, rang his bell in a jolly rhythm, grinning like a kid on Christmas morning.

"Aha," I said, "You aren't content with simply ding-a-linging like I am, are you?"

He chuckled and rang more heartily. "We may as well put some spirit into our ringing, have a little fun." And we did have fun. The minutes flew by like shooting stars.

But I couldn't manage to keep hold of my lovely golden bell. Perhaps I was concentrating more on chatting with the shoppers than snugly holding the bell. Perhaps the yarn of my mittens was too soft to allow a good grip. Perhaps I didn't want to clutch it too tightly for fear my hand would tire. For whatever reason, in the course of thirty short minutes, I dropped that bell seven times. Yes, seven.

No one seemed to notice the times Kevin was ringing alone. The kettle filled up with donations from warm-hearted individuals despite my bell-dropping. But I was embarrassed.

Although I laughed and teased Kevin that I was winning the game of "drop the bell," I couldn't help comparing those slippery fingers with my life. Every time that bell skittered across the pavement with a clang and a tinkle, it reminded me how often I drop the proverbial bell in my life. I snap at my husband. I avoid that less-than-kind lady at church. I criticize those I don't understand.

But like the shoppers joyfully depositing their money in the kettle even when I dropped the bell, God chooses to overlook my faults. He blesses my efforts to follow him despite the times I don't have a tight grip on his good plans for my life. He reminds me—like the bell—that none of us have to be perfect for him to make lovely music from our lives.

Jesus can use us regardless of our past sins, failures, and disabilities. If he waited for perfect people to do his work on the earth, nothing would get done. No matter how many times we need to pick up that dropped bell, he's there beside us, helping us to start over.

Then he puts his hand over ours and lovingly says, "Let's do this together. I believe in you."

—Jeanette

"The secret of change is to focus all your energy, not on fighting the old, but building the new."

—Socrates

Beauty-full Thoughts
In what ways have you dropped the bell?

_____

_____

_____

_____

Do you need to start over? God is there for you, waiting. He's not mad, disgusted, or shocked. He longs to help you because he loves you. On the lines below, write a prayer asking God for forgiveness and for his help as you pick up your bell.

_____

_____

_____

HELLO, BEAUTIFUL!

_____

_____

_____

23

I Promise

I came that they may have and enjoy life, and have it in abundance
[to the full, till it overflows]. (John 10:10 AMP)

When our nine-year-old daughter attended camp for the first time, she
worried about everything from making friends to what food they would
serve. Especially ham. Because ham was one of the few foods Esther hated,
she had a premonition they'd serve it.

"Don't worry, honey," I said. "Most Christian camps can't afford
expensive meats. *I promise you,* they won't serve ham."

While I helped Esther unpack the following weekend, I asked her how
she liked the food.

"Well, it was okay except the first night, Mom."

"Oh, what happened then?"

"They served *ham.*"

I was horrified that I'd broken my daughter's trust. I'd always prided
myself on following through with my word to my children so they'd feel
secure growing up. I also wanted to set an example of God's faithfulness.

But because I promised something I couldn't control, my promise was
worthless.

Although Esther readily forgave me—and this story became a family
joke—that was the last time I said "I promise" to her. And you'd think I
would've learned from that painful experience. Nope.

When our ten-year-old son, Ron, got an infected toe, he fretted that
the doctor would have to remove the toenail. This required, of course, a
dreaded shot.

I put my arm around his shoulder to reassure him. "Son, that's not
going to happen. All they'll do is examine your toe, then prescribe some

strong antibiotic to take the infection away. They won't give you a shot, *I promise.*"

Ron sat silent on the way to the podiatrist's office, his brown eyes clouded with dread. My reassurances of no shots bounced off his ears and thudded to the floorboards.

After the doctor examined Ron's cherry-colored toe, her perky demeanor changed. "I'm afraid we'll have to remove this toenail, young man. It's too infected to respond to a simple round of antibiotics."

Ron's face crumpled into tears. "Will I have to get a shot?" he said.

"I'm afraid so," the doctor said.

Although I held Ron's hand through the entire ugly ordeal and sang comforting songs to him, I felt like the heel of the century. For the second time, I'd let one of my kids down by making a promise I had no power to keep.

God doesn't worry about keeping his promises to us. Because he is eternal, he can control the outcome of his Word. When he says, "I promise," he comes through every time.

One of the promises God makes to us is that if we're in Christ, we're set free from the law of sin and death. By the power of the Holy Spirit, we can live upright lives. We have the right to say an emphatic no to sin and walk away from temptation. When we believe that promise and act on it, we can exercise victory over sin.

Jesus didn't come to earth, lay down his life, and conquer death to erase only the sins we committed before we were Christians. His power is at work in us now, every minute, so that we can enjoy the abundant, full life he mentioned in John 10:10—a life full of his beauty and grace.

God's love and grace aren't just for eternity. They'll work for you now in this life.

I promise.

—Jeanette

"Love is the beauty of the soul."
—St. Augustine

Beauty-full Thoughts

We've all made promises we couldn't keep, haven't we? God always keeps his promises. List as many of God's promises as you can think of:

HELLO, BEAUTIFUL!

_____

_____

_____

_____

_____

_____

_____

24

HIDING IN PLAIN SIGHT

Where can I go from your Spirit? Or where can I flee from your presence? If I go up to the heavens, you are there; if I make my bed in the depths, you are there. If I rise on the wings of the dawn, if I settle on the far side of the sea, even there your hand will guide me, and your right hand will hold me fast. (Psalm 139:7-10)

When I reached the doorway of the kitchen, I realized I was wearing nothing but my "big girl panties." I stopped, and no amount of persuasion from my mom would convince me to enter, not even my growling stomach.

I was three years old. Family friends had spent the night. When I awoke that morning, I could hear laughter wafting up the stairs to where I lay in my crib. So, I climbed over the side, pulled my blankie through the slats, and hurried down the stairs toward the fun sounds. But in my embarrassment that visitors might see me undressed, I stayed on the carpet outside the kitchen door. I thought I would remain unseen, invisible to the visitors inside the next room.

I smile now at the memory of my innocent childish belief. In reality, I was invisible to no one but myself. That thought led me to this one—how many times do I try to hide in plain sight and think no one can see my pain, my flaws, or my insecurities? Sometimes it works for a little while and people don't see through my smile of invisibility. But sooner than I realize, they do. I find that sometimes I still believe I can be invisible. I believe I can hide in plain sight.

I hate to admit, but I do it with God too. I think I can hide from my Creator, but God sees me. He sees us all as we truly are. He sees our pains and flaws and what we try to hide. And yet he loves us still. We can rest in the knowledge that we are seen and still completely, wholly, unconditionally loved today.

—Beth

"Never lose an opportunity of seeing anything beautiful, for beauty is God's handwriting."

—Ralph Waldo Emerson

Beauty-full Thoughts

What are you trying to hide from everyone including God? Write a prayer thanking God that he sees you—all of you—and loves you unconditionally.

_____

_____

_____

_____

_____

_____

_____

_____

25

One Step at a Time

For we are God's workmanship, created in Christ Jesus to do good works, which God prepared in advance for us to do. (Ephesians 2:10)

Noise and more noise. I glanced outside my window at work, wondering what was causing all the commotion. With a huge excavator-mounted jackhammer, a construction crew was breaking up the sidewalk across the street. That cement sidewalk must have been there for decades. But the workmen were busting it up in a few minutes, thanks to the stronger force of their jackhammer. The machine operator made his job look easy, sitting back in his cushy seat, a look of boredom on his face.

I thought of all the stubborn "sidewalks" in my life, the bad habits that have hounded me for decades. I wondered why overcoming my quick temper and impulsiveness is tougher to overcome than breaking up any amount of cement.

"It's not fair, Lord," I murmured. "I want to be a more patient, sensitive person than I am. I've prayed, cried, and begged you to help me grow up, but it seems like these habits are harder set than concrete. What's wrong with me?"

He gave me an answer, but not the one I expected.

Over the next few days as I witnessed the progress of the new sidewalk, I realized that breaking up the old cement was only a tiny part of the whole operation. Sometimes, the men would sit on the back of their truck or stand on the sidewalk for what seemed like hours, simply waiting. They couldn't go ahead with one part of the job until a previous task was at the proper stage. A friend told me they were putting in gas lines and meters, which proved that the job was bigger than it originally appeared.

Just as I thought the new sidewalk was perfect and ready for use, another crew came by to pour more concrete along the sides. Would it ever be finished?

The process reminded me of my life—every step slow, with lots of waiting between tiny spurts of progress. And much under-the-surface work that only a few people knew about. But instead of discouraging me, this thought inspired me not to give up on my seemingly tortoise-like progress.

"Thank you, Lord," I sighed. "I see I'm too impatient with you, wanting you to get rid of all my bad habits at once. But your plan is more like those construction workers, one step at a time. Help me to trust you during the process so I can enjoy my life, though I'm not perfect."

—Jeanette

"What lies behind us, and what lies before us are tiny matters compared to what lies within us."
—Ralph Waldo Emerson

Beauty-full Thoughts
What steps is God bringing you through right now to help you grow? People are like stained-glass windows. They sparkle and shine when the sun's out, but when the darkness sets in, their true beauty is revealed only if there's a light shining from within.

_____

_____

_____

_____

How can you practice more patience and embrace the process?

_____

_____

_____

_____

26

Broken Sheep

I am the Good Shepherd. I know my sheep and my sheep know me. (John 10:14)

I collect sheep. Not real ones. An assortment of resin, stuffed, and ceramic sheep sits on the large oak hutch in my living room. As I pass by them several times a day, they remind me of my dependence on the Lord and how he's promised to take care of me.

Recently, I noticed one of a matched pair had a broken leg. I don't even know how the accident happened and never found the missing piece. But when she's next to her sister, you hardly notice anything's wrong. She stands as straight as her twin whose legs are intact. I like to think she gained strength and confidence from her sister by standing alongside her.

Are you broken? If you said yes, then good for you. I say yes to brokenness too. We're all broken in one place ... or ten. And when we readily admit it, we're on our way to finding the help we need to become whole.

In order to restore and heal us, Jesus our Good Shepherd, often puts us in a group of other Christians who will love us. These fellow sheep, like the twin in my hutch who stands next to her sister, hold us up. They may pray for us and with us. They may give us ideas of methods that helped them heal. They may share Bible verses or passages that changed their thinking and helped them believe the Good Shepherd's love for them.

When a broken sheep is alone, you can spot her right away. She seems smaller and more vulnerable. But when she's close to another, stronger sheep, her flaws are less visible. By working, loving, and sharing together, we help each other heal in all those broken places we may not even be aware of. We can bring out the hidden beauty in a fellow sheep.

We need each other. Let's come alongside a broken sister or brother today and say, "I love you. I'm here for you. It doesn't matter how you got broken. You're beautiful to Jesus and to me, and he and I will help you heal."

—Jeanette

"A friend is one that knows you as you are, understands where you have been, accepts what you have become, and still, gently allows you to grow."
—Anonymous

Beauty-full Thoughts
Are you broken?
List some friends you can stand near to gain strength from.

_____

_____

_____

_____

_____

_____

List some friends you can be strong for.

_____

_____

_____

_____

_____

_____

27

TODAY'S JOY

So do not worry about tomorrow; for tomorrow will care for itself. Each day has enough trouble of its own. (Matthew 6:34 NASB)

If you're anything like me, you need to remind yourself that God knows what he's doing. He's committed to our care, and no matter what comes he'll be there, making a way where there seems to be no way. Ways to keep us safe, feel secure in our beautiful selves, and believe we are loved for who we are.

I want to see
Tomorrow and tomorrow and
Forever.
To plan my way,
To fix the broken
Before it breaks.
But then I remember
I am not You.
And if tomorrow
Never comes
I've wasted the joy
Of today.

—Jeanette

"Beauty is not in the face; beauty is a light in the heart."
—Kahlil Gibran

Beauty-full Thoughts

List three of your worries:

_____

_____

_____

_____

List three ways you can find joy despite those worries:

_____

_____

_____

_____

28

Never Forgotten

Never will I leave you; never will I forsake you. (Hebrews 13:5)

Last year on my birthday, I received several cards, calls, texts, and gifts from family and friends, making the day special to me.

But this year felt different. Lonely. Ordinary. The phone didn't ring. No cards came in the mail. I felt forgotten. My birthday was merely another Monday.

I started a load of laundry and then swept the kitchen floor of the weekend's accumulated food crumbs and dust bunnies. Sitting in front of the computer and opening up Quicken software, I prepared to pay bills and reconcile the checkbook, my normal Monday tasks. I figured I'd fix myself a grilled cheese sandwich for lunch.

Then the phone rang. "Happy birthday!" my friend Susan said cheerfully. "Do you have birthday lunch plans?"

"Actually, I don't have any plans today." I tried to hide the disappointment in my voice.

"Really?" She sounded surprised. "Can I take you out to lunch?"

Instantly, my day transformed from a blah to special. And my whole attitude about my birthday changed and lifted my mood. I suddenly felt loved.

We met at a favorite local café, and I savored every bite of my comforting chicken pot pie. Susan and I caught up on what we were reading, writing down each other's recommendations for our to-be-read lists. We talked about our kids, jobs, and what new insights we were learning in our devotional times. I left the restaurant with a full belly and an even fuller heart, carrying in my hand the new book Susan had given me. I said a prayer of thanksgiving for my friend.

Have you ever had a day when you felt forgotten? It's painful, isn't it? Did someone sweep in at the last minute and show you that you mattered to them? Or are you still longing for someone to show they care?

Sometimes, all it would take to turn a disappointing day around is for a friend to send a text, someone to smile as they pass by, or to receive a card of encouragement. Suddenly, we feel seen. And that changes everything.

In those lonely moments, it's easy to forget we aren't alone. God is always with us. My favorite verse is, *Never will I leave you. Never will I forsake you* (Hebrews 13:5). Even if a friend doesn't call and ask us out to eat and we spend the day alone, God is with us.

—Beth

"How beautiful a day can be when kindness touches it!"
—George Elliston

As you color this verse, ask God to show you his presence.

Never will I
leave you;
never will I
forsake you.
Hebrews 13:5 NIV

29

Encourage Me, Please!

Therefore encourage one another and build up one another, just as you also are doing. (Thessalonians 5:11 NASB)

"Everyone, Valerie is feeling kind of down today and asked me to announce that she would appreciate any and all hugs, happy words, and prayers you'd like to share with her."

The leader of the weight-control club I attend ended a recent meeting with this announcement. My first response was that Valerie was really brave to admit to everyone here that she's down. Then I realized that's actually the way we ought to act in our support systems. We should openly share when we need encouragement, rather than braving the storms alone. My admiration for Valerie rocketed as I got in line to give her a hug.

I think of all the times I'd felt discouraged and ready to give up on myself. Mostly, I whined to my husband or a friend. Occasionally, I ask the Lord to send me some encouragement, and the results always amaze me.

Sometimes God sends a friend to say, "I love your writing," or "You make everyone feel comfortable around you." Other times he's prompted me to turn on the radio at the exact moment an uplifting song was playing. A cup of excellent coffee, a goat prancing in a field, a tree vibrant with red and orange leaves in the fall, a card in the mail from a faraway friend, a silly joke—all have encouraged me at one time or another.

Not everyone possesses the same kind of courage as Valerie. But we can always go to the Lord when our spirits are low. Not only does he understand, Isaiah 53:3 calls him a *man of sorrows*. He wants to give us the reassurance we need.

God is as willing to encourage you as he does Valerie, me, Beth, and every other woman who feels like she's sinking. He has millions of methods up his sleeves for custom-made ways to say, he loves you and is there for you. He wants to tell you that you're valuable, capable, and lovable. Don't give up on yourself. You'll come through this.

Just ask.

—Jeanette

"Never give up, for that is just the place and time that the tide will turn."

—Harriet Beecher Stowe

Beauty-full Thoughts
Who do you feel safe asking for support?

_____

_____

_____

_____

How would you like the Lord to encourage you in your stressful, sad times?

_____

_____

_____

_____

_____

_____

Just ask.

30

Princess

For in Christ all the fullness of the Deity lives in bodily form, and you have been given fullness in Christ, who is the head over every power and authority. (Colossians 2:9-10)

Sometimes we need to flat-out ask God, "How do you see me? Why do you love—even like—me? What in me makes you happy?" There's nothing arrogant or prideful in this request. As women, you and I need affirmation of our worth. Humans don't always do the greatest job of showing us our value. They're broken too. But God views you and me with eyes of a perfect parent, one who would and did give everything for us. God's not mad at you or me. He's not sorry we're part of his family. He treasures us and wants the best for us.

You are beautiful.
You are lovely.
You are good,
Growing to be a queen
Who reigns and rules
With a scepter of righteousness.
Don't turn back to the rags of despair
That clothed you before,
Keeping you chained
To people's opinions.
They know nothing of me
And the wealth I've invested in you,
My princess, my beloved, my betrothed.
Go forward, your head held high,
Your eyes bright with hope.

For I have called you
My own.
That is all you need.
I have crowned you with honor and glory.
I have promised you
A place at my banquet.
And once I've decided who will attend,
Satan himself cannot
Erase your name
From the guest list.
So, come sit with me on my throne.
Laugh with me, dance with me,
Let me tell you my secret things,
And be free.
—Jeanette

"When virtue and modesty enlighten her charms, the lustre of a beautiful woman is brighter than the stars of heaven ..."
—Akhenaton

Beauty-full Thoughts
As you read this poem, highlight the lines that stand out.

If you like, write your own poem from Jesus's point of view, telling you how he values and loves you.

_____

_____

_____

_____

_____

_____

_____

_____

_____

31

Suit Yourself

Yet you, Lord, are our Father. We are the clay, you are the potter;
we are all the work of your hand. (Isaiah 64:8)

For my sixteenth birthday, my parents bought me an expensive new
outfit to wear when Mom and I accompanied Dad to the church he was
preaching at that Sunday. I felt classy in the navy wool skirt and matching
jacket. I didn't care much about what other teenagers at those churches
thought about how I dressed. I was mature-looking, like a college kid or
a rich girl. I was important. To accentuate the outfit, I added a cream,
long-sleeved blouse, blue hose, and blue flats. I was blue from my neck to
my toes. I loved how I looked. It fit the image I wanted to portray to the
world ... on the outside.

But on the inside, I didn't fit in at all. I was the new girl. Every Sunday
felt like starting the school year in a new town. I bravely attended the teen
Sunday School class, carrying a tiny, worn Bible and sat quietly, answering
when called on, yet praying I never was. I wanted to be the new girl that
everyone fell in love with. Instead, I was the shy, weirdo in the corner.

Because my dad preached, I heard the same sermon on many of those
Sundays. My favorite one described how God is the potter and we are the
clay.

"This is the word that came to Jeremiah from the Lord: 'Go down
to the potter's house, and there I will give you my message.' So
I went down to the potter's house, and I saw him working at
the wheel. But the clay was marred in his hands; so the potter
formed it into another pot, shaping it as seemed best to him.
Then the word of the Lord came to me. He said, 'Can I not do
with you, Israel, as this potter does?' Declares the Lord. 'Like

clay in the hand of the potter, so are you in my hand, Israel.'"
(Jeremiah 18:1-6)

Over the weeks, I heard my dad talking about a God who forms us as he sees fit. I began to fall in love with this God who created me and still forms me like a piece of pottery into exactly what he designed me to be. With my beautiful wool suit, my outside may have looked perfect, but inside God was quietly, gently working to make me into something useful.

I look back at that frightened girl who wondered if God could use her and am in awe at how God has worked. Despite my insecurities, my introversion, my desire to appear perfect on the outside, God has been and still is at work. Today, he's using my written words. He uses my hands to create knitted gifts for those I love. He uses my food to feed my neighbor. He uses what I've learned through brokenness, failures, and grief to help me encourage others in similar situations.

I wanted to come across as perfect, as beautiful and important, but God has made me useful, not despite my flaws and imperfections, but because of them. What an encouragement to know that God is molding us into the shape he sees as best for us.

—Beth

"Life isn't about finding yourself. Life is about creating yourself."
—George Bernard Shaw

Beauty-full Thoughts
Is there an area of your life that looks broken or flawed? Ask God to make that area useful to him.

_____

_____

_____

_____

_____

_____

32

Running with Grief

But you, God, see the trouble of the afflicted; you consider their grief and take it in hand. The victims commit themselves to you; you are the helper of the fatherless. (Psalm 10:14)

A few months after my mother died, I had a sudden urge to run. I'd never before felt that urge even though I did track and field all through middle and high school. Basically, I ran only as much as the coach made me before I headed down to the high jump mat for the rest of practice. I hated running. It made my side, legs, and lungs hurt. Jogging was the torture I went through to get to jump over a pole, which I loved. I loved soaring through the air and seeing how high I could get off the ground.

Suddenly, here I was, in my late forties and wanting to feel the wind on my face as I ran as fast and as far as my wimpy legs could take me. I wanted to push my muscles to the limit and feel the soreness the next day. That pain felt like it had a purpose, unlike the agony that filled my heart from missing my mom. Still, I kept running.

Running became therapy for me, my time alone with God. My body became stronger and my heart, nourished. The beauty of God's creation reminded me of God's daily presence. I saw evidence of God at work as I ran down country roads. Each morning, I stuffed a giant bandana in the pocket of my hoodie and ran. When tears fell, I wiped them with the bandana. I felt the Lord's presence with me as I cried and ran.

I searched the gravel road daily for a pebble that stood out. When I found the right one, I would reach down and pick it up. I'd rub its smooth edges against my thumb, feeling the glass-like hardness and remembering God was my rock. As my collection of running rocks grew, my strength grew. I saw hope and a new path for my future. God whispered words of hope into my ears and placed a new vision before my eyes.

I learned that when I feel pain, God is waiting to take a run with me.

What direction are you running? Are you running from your pain or with your pain toward Jesus?

—Beth

"There is no remedy for love than to love more."
—Henry David Thoreau

Beauty-full Thoughts
Journal below about your grief.

_____

_____

_____

_____

_____

Now spend a few moments in prayer asking God for his strength, peace, and presence in your situation. Write your prayer below, if you wish.

_____

_____

_____

_____

_____

_____

_____

33

BRUISED BUT BEAUTIFUL

A bruised reed he will not break, and a smoldering wick he will not snuff out. In faithfulness he will bring forth justice. (Isaiah 42:3)

Stupid. Inept. Ditzy. These are the messages I grew up with. As a child, I lacked the discernment to understand that instead of declaring truth, the adults in my life were expressing their frustration at innocent, childish acts.

I tried to compensate for my lack of confidence by seeking to please teachers, classmates, and youth leaders. Although I gained many friends with this method, how I saw myself changed little. In my mind, I was still the clueless little redhead who needed a map from the living room to the kitchen.

Whenever I'd make a silly mistake, I drew attention to it, laughing at myself before others had the chance to say, "I can't believe you did that!" or "What were you thinking?"

Not until I was in my forties, after I had raised two remarkable kids and graduated college with a perfect GPA, did I realize that I'm not dumb after all. I'm smart. And I've been listening to lies all my life.

Please don't assume that once this revelation dawned on me, I found it easy to think of myself accurately. In order to change my self-talk, I had to work harder than a shoe clerk assisting a centipede. I still struggle at times. When someone explains in great detail a concept I already understand, those feelings of incompetence resurface and echo through my soul. I must fight to gain control over the deep-seated lies that tell me I'm less than precious in God's sight.

My most powerful weapon? God's Word. I speak it aloud to myself and to Satan, the author of lies. I mediate on Scripture until his lovely truths overshadow my doubts. I listen to it via songs that reflect God's heart brimming with love and esteem for me. One of those songs, *Bruised Reeds,* was written by my husband, Kevin, during a bleak time of self-doubt in his life. Isaiah 42:3 shows Jesus as One who lifts up the broken and bruised and draws out their true beauty in the light of his justice.

If, like me, your soul is black and blue, if you are weary and wounded, let the words of this song bring healing and truth to you. Let Jesus make your crooked places straight. Instead of listening to the echoes of your past, choose to believe in his truth about you. That you are valuable, lovable, and capable. You might be bruised, but in his eyes you're beautiful.

Bruised Reeds
© 1990 Kevin Don Levellie
He won't wound the weary, he calls them to rest;
He calls them to comfort now upon his breast.
The soul that is worried, the fearful of heart,
Shall not be excluded from all he imparts.
He shall not break bruised reeds,
Or extinguish the smoldering spark,
He shall make strong the weak, give life to their flame.
He shall not fail nor be discouraged in anything,
Though they tread a path unknown he makes it straight.
He won't leave the faint ones, he urges them on,
He cheers as they run the race and points them beyond.
Though courage is broken, though purpose is weak,
He's been in their place and can patiently lead.

—Jeanette

"Dare to be what you are and learn to resign with a good grace all that you are not and to believe in your own individuality."
—Henri Fredric Amiel

Beauty-full Thoughts
What bruises from your past have caused you to believe lies about yourself?

_____

_____

_____

_____

_____

_____

_____

_____

_____

In what ways can you replace those lies with the truth of how God views you?

_____

_____

_____

_____

_____

34

Trying Too Hard

And he has said to me, "My grace is sufficient for you, for power is perfected in weakness." Most gladly, therefore, I will rather boast about my weaknesses, so that the power of Christ may dwell in me. (2 Corinthians 12:9 NASB)

Sometimes, when I'm in the midst of a troubling or worrisome circumstance, I have a hard time speaking my thoughts to the Lord. So, I journal my prayers. Then I listen and write beneath my words what I believe the Lord is telling me in response to my usually anguished cries on the page. I don't mean I hear an audible voice from God. But down inside, like the sweet wisdom of a dear friend or beloved parent, I *hear* the voice of my Shepherd.

Several years ago, during a time of discouragement, this is what my journal looked like:

Lord, I need encouragement today. I really don't want to go by my feelings or I wouldn't have a good day at all. I know I have to choose joy and choose to have peace rather than turmoil, but I need your help even in the choosing. I need you to show me what to do and how to think in order to choose joy rather than sorrow. And I need you to send me encouragement because right now I just don't care about anything. To care would mean work, and I'd rather rest and sleep and escape.

And this is what I believe I sensed the Lord telling me:

Jeanette, I don't want *you* to care. *I* will care for you. When *you* take care, it means you aren't giving me a chance to help you and care for you. You are trying to do life yourself and that's pride. When you let go and relax, my Spirit takes over and gets the job done in an almost effortless way. You know it's me at work in you when you don't have to struggle to get something and struggle to keep it. For me to carry you, you need to simply relax and not wiggle down and run off. Trusting me means allowing *me* to carry you. *Just quit trying so hard.*

I don't know about you, but I have a difficult time allowing Jesus to carry me. Somewhere down inside me is a little girl who still reels over the abandonment of her daddy when she was six, who grew up thinking she needed to take care of herself or no one else would. I suppose modern psychology would call that a "trust issue." So, okay. I have a trust issue with my heavenly Father at times.

When all heck is breaking loose in my health or my family, to simply rest in the love of God and believe that Jesus is going to see me through to victory takes more faith and maturity than I think I possess.

But that's one of the most wonderful aspects of God's nature. He sees what he made us to be—complete in him, according to Colossians 2:10—not what we view from our puny perspective. Because of his mighty Holy Spirit in us, the Lord knows that we *can* trust, we *can* rest, and we *can* believe, even when we feel helpless and weak. He believes in us more than we believe in ourselves.

I probably will be tempted to always try to solve my own problems and fix my own hurts. So, I need those constant reminders from Jesus that my success in life doesn't rely on my trying. His grace is enough.

—Jeanette

"Be yourself not a copy of others."
—Anonymous

Beauty-full Thoughts
As you color this picture to look like you, remember God is carrying you today.

35

GRACE AND GLORY

A person's wisdom yields patience; it is to one's glory to overlook an offense. (Proverbs 19:11)

"Viola confided in me that her stepbrother raped her when she was eight years old. I'm not sure anyone else—even your grandpa—knew that."

I stared at my Grandma Viola's best friend, Joy, who'd invited me out to lunch following Grandma's funeral. I dropped my fork to the table. My mouth flapped open. But I couldn't make any sound come out of it.

Joy reached across the table and covered my cold hand with her warm one. "I'm sorry if I upset you, Jeanette. I never meant to do that. But I've carried this secret around with me for decades, and now that Viola's gone, I felt it was safe to get it off my chest."

Finally, I managed to choke out a few words. "That would explain the haunted, empty look in her eyes in the one photo we have of her as a child. I feel like crying every time I look at that picture."

"In the early nineteen hundreds, girls who were taken advantage of like that had little recourse. I'm sure Viola simply had to do her best to avoid trouble and not make life more miserable than it already was. Her stepmother would never have believed her own son capable of rape."

I recalled the stories my mom had told me of Grandma's upbringing by a harsh stepmother after her mom died. The trips to the dump to get raggedy clothes and mismatched shoes for school. The cruel treatment of her and her natural brother while her stepbrothers received special favors. The growling of her belly day after day from lack of sufficient food. And finally, when she was seventeen, marrying the first man who showed an interest in her in order to escape the prison of her home life.

"One time she said that she'd forgiven her stepbrother, Grayson, of what she called their growing up years," I told Joy, my voice still shaky. "I thought she meant the kinds of tiffs all siblings get into. Now I see it was much more than that. Wow!"

"Yet Viola was the sweetest person you'd ever want to meet. And I'm not just saying that because she was my best friend. Everyone who knew her for five minutes or five decades said the same thing."

I'd said it myself many times. Grandma exuded grace and acceptance to everyone she met, regardless of their differing opinions or how they treated her. She was never without a kind word or a reassuring smile.

"Sometimes your grandpa would make her so mad she'd come over to my house and bang on my door, telling me she needed to get away from 'that unreasonable man,'" Joy said between laughs. "You know how your grandpa had to have everything his way. But by the next morning, she'd have forgotten all about their disagreement. She was mercy and forgiveness personified."

I nodded, once again silent. I'd known many people who'd experienced less horror and fewer hardships than Grandma had, yet they were bitter and merciless. What made the difference?

I thought of the writer of Proverbs saying that insightful people restrain their anger and overlook offenses (see Proverbs 19:11). Knowing Grandma's forgiving nature, I believe I can safely say she made a decision every day to walk in glory, to overlook offenses and wrongs, and to forgive her abusers. Rather than clinging to the pain of the past, she chose to walk into the future covered in grace. It was a decision that brought her glory.

Some of the hardest words we utter are "I forgive you," whether we say them to a person's face or silently in our hearts. Yet, they're the words that will set us free from bitterness and bondage. They take us from harshness to honor. They'll give us the same kind of glory that Grandma had, a glory that made her beautiful.

—Jeanette

"The best part of beauty which no picture can express."
—Francis Bacon

Beauty-full Thoughts
Ask God to bring anyone to mind you may need to forgive.

_____

_____

_____

_____

Write a prayer asking God to help you learn to forgive the person(s) you listed above.

_____

_____

_____

_____

_____

_____

36

Stolen Dreams

Trust in and rely confidently on the Lord with all your heart and do not rely on your own insight or understanding. In all your ways know and acknowledge and recognize Him, and he will make your paths straight and smooth. (Proverbs 3:5-6 AMP)

I took a bite of my salad as I listened to Abby tell me about a woman at church who was leading a dynamic Bible study where fifty women attended. She described how this woman believed God had spoken to her about writing a book and had even given her a title and a subject. Seven months later, she'd completed the book. Within a week of finishing the book, she had a publisher and book deal. Abby went on and on about how wonderfully God was working in this woman's life.

I felt a stab of hot jealousy in my chest. I thought, *Why God? Why are you giving my dreams to her?*

As I took stock of my life thus far, I gave myself a failing grade. Yes, I have a writing degree. But my Bible study group consists of three other women from church. Only three women! Few people at my large church even know my name, let alone sign up for my group. I have a bachelor's degree, but no career. I'm just a mom. Why would anyone be interested in what I have to say? The ugly monster of comparison took over my brain and emotions, and my appetite left the room.

Look what you have to show for the thousands of dollars' worth of education. See how no one flocks to your group? You must be a bad leader. You're boring, too old, too quiet, and shy. You should be more charismatic. You're not good enough for God to use.

Then, almost instantly, I heard the gentle, loving voice of God tell me, *I am big enough to use both of you. All I ask of you is that you be grateful for what I'm doing in everyone's life, not in yours alone. Can you thank me for using this other woman instead of tearing yourself down?* He reminded me that when I trusted him rather than my own perceptions, he would smooth my path. *I am using you, Beth. Only not in the way you planned.*

That was a hard lunch and a hard lesson for me. God wants to use me, as he wants to use each of us. Sometimes we may have paths similar to those of others, but God is big enough to use all of us if we're willing to follow his plan. And that plan can fill us with hope even as we question how he is using others.

—Beth

"The fountain of beauty is the heart and every generous thought illustrates the walls of your chamber."
—Francis Quarles

Beauty-full Thoughts

When we compare ourselves to others, sometimes we feel defeated or like a failure. But God is at work in each of us. Instead of concentrating on what God's doing in another's life, think about how God is using you, or could use you. Write down three ways you see God at work in your life.

_____

_____

_____

_____

_____

_____

37

You Love Me Just As I Am

Therefore, accept one another, just as Christ also accepted us to the glory of God. (Romans 15:7 NASB)

During a time of prayer when I struggled to forgive myself—a common occurrence decades ago—I wrote my first song. It simply flowed out as I sang to the Lord what I believed he was trying to get through to me from the moment I was born anew at age eight … that he loved me unconditionally.

> You love me just as I am, Lord.
> You love me just as I am, Lord.
> You see deep inside me and look past my faults
> And You love me just as I am.
> You need me just as I am, Lord.
> You need me just as I am, Lord.
> My value to you can't be measured by man
> And You need me just as I am.
> You use me just as I am, Lord.
> You use me just as I am, Lord.
> You filled me with your Holy Spirit and power
> And You use me just as I am.

Our family traveled and sang at many different churches during this time, and soon we featured my song in our programs. We sang the last verse to the audience, and then had them turn and sing it to one another.

> I love you just as you are.
> I love you just as you are.

Because Jesus loves me just as I am

I love you just as you are.

The reactions were as varied as the audience members. Some people couldn't manage to make eye contact with anyone near them while singing. Others laughed nervously. But some—very few, really—sang it with feeling and misty eyes. Occasionally, if I was speaking for a ladies' group, I'd ask them to close their eyes, pretend they were looking in the mirror, and sing the words to themselves. Now that's challenging. We're not used to saying I love you to ourselves. Why is that?

We're taught from toddlerhood that we need to share our toys and snacks, let others go first, set aside our wants, do the noble thing. And we should do all those. They are biblical principles and eternal truths. Yet somehow—unless you were raised by different people than I was—our parents, teachers, and mentors failed to give us the balanced approach of Jesus's viewpoint. Every one of us has equal value in God's eyes. He loves us all the same. We aren't the most important person on earth, and no one else is more important than we are.

So, it's okay to love ourselves because Jesus loves us just as we are.

That doesn't mean we can hurt anyone we please, say whatever mean insult is on our mind, and walk away thinking, *I'm good. God loves me just as I am. Deal with it.*

It does mean we're kind to ourselves, forgiving ourselves when we mess up, caring for our own needs as we would anyone else. Psychologists call this *self-care*, which is a healthy way of putting value on the unique individual God made us to be, loving ourselves as we love others like Jesus taught.

Self-care won't make you more beautiful to God. He already loves you exactly as you are. But it may help you see the boundless beauty hidden in your soul. It may enable you to follow those dreams you've set aside for years. It may give you the courage to look in the mirror and say, "I love you."

—Jeanette

"Imagination disposes of everything; it creates beauty, justice, and happiness, which are everything in this world."

—Blaise Pascal

Beauty-full Thoughts

Write "I Love You!" on a sticky note and put it on your bathroom mirror, refrigerator door, or somewhere else where you'll see it every day.

Every time you see those words, say them.

38

Puddles of Gold

Praise be the God and Father of our Lord Jesus Christ, the Father of compassion and the God of all comfort, who comforts us in all our troubles, so that we can comfort those in any trouble with the comfort we ourselves have received from God. (2 Corinthians 1:3-4)

My friend Deidre emailed me with a request to pray for her upcoming appointment to have a root canal. I knew she'd had some extensive dental work done less than a month earlier, so I asked her if perhaps her dentist had overlooked something in his examination. After explaining the dentist's rationale, her next comment surprised me.

"Praise God I have an emergency fund. And I haven't had to spend much on dental work for several years, so I can't complain."

Wow! How does Deidre keep such a positive outlook, always finding something good in the predicaments the devil throws at her?

I knew she had experienced abuse from her mom and ex-spouse, which, for most of us, would've caused a low self-esteem. Yet, she had cultivated a positive mindset she called a life approach of always looking on the bright side. She'd once shared with me how she trained herself.

"The looking-for-gold-in-life's-puddles approach is definitely something I've chosen to do. Along the way, the Lord has exposed me to positive-minded speakers and authors. I've been working on it a long time."

I felt better when I learned Deidre wasn't born with a sunny outlook. She had cultivated her excellent attitude over the span of several decades. That gave me hope for my own outlook toward all the unexpected, negative twists the road of my own life had taken.

I'm sure this is true of your life as well. Relationships and situations rarely turn out the way we originally envision them.

The dream marriage that turned into a nightmare.

The ideal job we lost to someone else or got laid off from.

The flourishing ministry that withered and died, leaving us disillusioned.

The close friendship that cracked and finally splintered into a hundred pieces.

The excellent health we once enjoyed is being swallowed by illness.

Shattered dreams can lead to disappointment. Disappointment is the thief of joy and hope. It mires us in remorse. When remorse shows up at our doorstep, we're tempted to blame God, others, and ourselves—my default—when things don't turn out the way we expect.

Or we can adopt Deidre's go-to plan of finding a way to repurpose the unexpected, negative outcome into a blessing. How do we do this?

We can start by asking God to give us his thoughts on the matter. "How do you see this, Father? I can't find a thing to praise you about here. Can you please shed some light on this dark spot?"

Once we open the door to his limitless wisdom, we can expect ideas to pop up—sometimes immediately, sometimes later—that will help us see the gold flakes in the puddle.

If our puddle is	*We might find this kind of gold:*
Our marriage ended in divorce.	We possess sensitivity to someone else experiencing the same kind of anguish. We've learned what to look for in a future spouse.
We lost out on a job we wanted or were let go.	We can thank God for the experience we gained and learn from them for the next job.
A ministry we loved ended.	We can appreciate what we learned and how we grew during this ministry, preparing us for a better one in the future.
A close-knit relationship fell apart.	We have learned what warning signs to look for in a relationship and what to avoid.

Sickness plagues our days.	We realize how we took our health for granted and will never do that again. Our compassion has increased for others who are sick.

Let's not allow discouragement to get the better of us as we're learning this technique. Long-standing mindsets and family traditions of worry and whining have deep roots. But each baby step we take toward changing our outlook will empower us to rise above the puddles and operate in the gold standard of God's viewpoint.

—Jeanette

"The essence of all beautiful art, is gratitude."
—Friedrich Nietzsche

Beauty-full Thoughts

My current puddles:	I might find this kind of Gold:

39

There All the Time

For he chose us in him before the creation of the world to be
holy and blameless in his sight. (Ephesians 1:4)

"Sorry we're late, Robert!" I ran into the farm store where we were
scheduled to ring the Salvation Army bell. Since my husband, Kevin, and
I had so much fun manning the red kettle the previous year, we decided to
add this activity to our permanent list of Christmas experiences.

Robert took off his apron and handed it and the bell to me. As I slipped
the apron over my head, I looked around the tidy entryway where smiling
shoppers came and went. "Is there only one apron and one bell?"

"I guess so. This is all I saw when I got here."

"Hmmm ... we had two last year." I wondered if the shoppers would be
confused. How would it look if only one of us were wearing the traditional
red apron and ringing the bell while the other stood idly by?

When Kevin breezed in from parking the car, I explained the situation.
He too glanced around the small room, searching for another apron and
bell. "Well, how about this? You can wear the apron and I'll ring the bell."

I laughingly agreed to his half-and-half solution. But I felt odd standing
there with no bell in my hand as if I wasn't fully doing my job.

None of the shoppers seemed to notice our little dilemma. They were
cheerful as they generously stuffed bills or clinked coins into the gleaming
red kettle. One lady taught her small son how to fold his money in a tiny
wad to fit into the slot.

Other shoppers returned our greeting of "Merry Christmas!" as they
gave from their hearts. The time zoomed by.

Our shift was the final one of the day. When Ken, our area's Salvation Army treasurer, came to pick up the brimming kettle, he looked at my empty hands. "Didn't you have another bell?"

"No, and we only had one apron too, so we divided them."

He reached over to a sack sitting in plain view on the deep windowsill and opened it to reveal several aprons and bells.

"What?" I cried, trying to fake a laugh as my face heated with embarrassment. "How could we have missed that?"

"We always provide at least two aprons and bells. I see three here. But don't worry; you did fine coming up with a solution." Ken acted graciously toward us.

On the way home, I said to Kevin, "We could have both worn aprons and rang two bells after all. Those extras were right under our noses. I feel like an idiot."

"Don't worry, Jeanette." His voice was gentle as he reached for my hand. "We'll know where to look next year." Kevin's kind words eased my feelings of self-consciousness and encouraged me that I didn't need to repeat the same mistake in the future.

Much like Jesus.

I fret about silly things like not having both an apron and a bell, what people will think of me if my purse doesn't match my shoes, or if my lipstick is too dark.

I also worry about enormous mistakes and sins of my past, whether they took place twenty-five years or twenty minutes ago. I'm afraid that a stupid decision or a wrong choice will ruin my future or the lives of those I love.

Enter Jesus, with loving words to reassure me that I'm not too far gone for his grace to redeem every one of my lousy decisions and besetting sins. He reminds me that before I was born—even before the world began—he called me to be holy and blameless in his sight. He also holds my future in his loving embrace. I don't have worry that I'll spoil everything because Jesus will never give up on me or quit believing in me.

Like the missing bell, he's been there all the time. And he's not going anywhere.

—Jeanette

"Though we travel the world to find the beautiful, we must carry it with us or we find it not."

—Ralph Waldo Emerson

Beauty-full Thoughts

Are you caught up in trying to be perfect? God wants to redeem your imperfection. Why not share this pain with him and ask him to redeem your mistakes and sins? Then write out your thoughts and requests for him to help you relax in who you are.

_____

_____

_____

_____

_____

_____

40

You Are Stronger Than You Think

Let perseverance finish its work so that you may be mature and complete, not lacking anything. (James 1:4)

I stood behind my craft fair table, trying to be bubbly and cheerful like the vendor next to me. But inside, I was a quivering mess. Would anyone want to buy my hand-knitted hats? I'd spent many hours making them, and I loved them. They were soft, warm, beautiful winter hats with the cutest faux fur pompoms on top. At least that was how I described them in my head. But my mouth refused to work.

I smiled awkwardly at every person who stopped by to try on one. And with each purchase, I worried that they would get home and decide they didn't like the hat or find some fault with them. I worried they would be too big or too small or not wear well over time.

As the morning progressed, so did my fears. *Maybe I should give them away. Should I really be taking money? I'm not a professional, for Pete's sake!* By the end of the day, I was exhausted from fake smiling and trying to act confident.

That night I went home and thought about the day. People had actually bought hats, and even those who didn't buy commented on their quality. I thought back to how much fun I'd had knitting all of them as I told myself, "Today you must knit. That's your job for the day." I'd felt ridiculously indulgent to sit and knit hour after hour during the weeks leading up to the craft fair. I realized selling hats hadn't been as much about selling, but more about creating. I spent a month doing what I love to do, and the knitting fueled my soul.

So, how did I reconcile the two different parts of the project—the making and the selling? Making was a joy, while selling was a torture. What

I learned from the experience is that everything worthwhile is comprised of fun-filled parts and difficult, necessary parts. I also learned that persevering when necessary in order to do the thing you were created to do can boost your self-esteem and bring you joy.

Why? Because our feelings are fickle. Feelings allow negative self-talk to invade our thinking. They tell us we can't meet challenges, precisely because they're hard. They tell us that if something is tough, we're not meant to do it.

The Bible doesn't say that. It tells us in James 1:4 that perseverance leads to maturity.

If we keep going when we feel like something is too much for us to handle, we'll discover we're stronger than we thought. Could that strength come from God?

—Beth

"The question is not what you look at, but what you see."
—Henry David Thoreau

Beauty-full Thoughts

What is something you want to do but don't because it seems too easy, too indulgent? Could God want to use the talent that comes easily to you?

_____

_____

Journal about a time that was really difficult. Think about the ways God helped you through that time. Take some time to thank God for his strength that helped you to do what you didn't think you could do.

_____

_____

_____

_____

_____

_____

_____

What is something you want to do but don't because it seems too hard?

_____

_____

_____

_____

Ask God if he wants to use this to strengthen you and show you ways his strength lives in you. Then stand up straight, look in the mirror and say, "Hello, Beautiful!"

_____

_____

_____

_____

BONUS CHAPTER

Hope for a Poor Self-Image

The Lord your God is with you, he is mighty to save. He will take great delight in you, he will quiet you with his love, he will rejoice over you with singing. (Zephaniah 3:17)

When I first met Judy, a new employee at my workplace, I couldn't identify why I liked her so much. Was it her ready laughter, her openness to share struggles as well as joys, her ability to make me feel important? Then one day as I overheard Judy admonish a teenage employee and make the correction sound helpful, I understood what made her appealing. Judy liked herself. After decades and several jobs later, I look back and realize how rare Judy's healthy self-esteem was.

Most of us can count on one hand the people we know who exude confidence. The majority of our acquaintances—even fellow Christians—suffer from varying degrees of insecurity.

Poor self-image is not a new malady, nor is it unique to modern-day Americans. Adam and Eve hid from the Lord when they realized they were naked after eating forbidden fruit. Both the stuttering Moses and the teenage Jeremiah tried to talk God out of using them as spiritual leaders. Even the apostle Peter, after he followed the Lord's command and experienced a miraculous catch of fish, stated that he felt unworthy to be in the presence of God.

In nearly all cultures and in every era, people have suffered from feelings of insecurity, uncertainty, anxiety, worthlessness, or self-hatred.

Even those we expect to possess a healthy view of themselves—ones born with natural beauty, talent, intelligence, or wealth—don't always smile when they look in the mirror.

Superstar Mariah Carey told an interviewer, "I've always had really low self-esteem, and I still do."

The late Maya Angelou, an award-winning writer, admitted, "I have written eleven books, but each time I think, 'Uh-oh, they're going to find out now. I've run a game on everybody, and they're going to find me out.'"

President Abraham Lincoln, whom many consider a brilliant leader, suffered with bouts of depression and panic attacks.

While not everyone with a poor self-image acts the same, many exhibit these similar behaviors:

- Extremes in Body Language

People who don't see themselves in a positive light often slouch, hang their head, make little or no eye contact, and rarely speak up. Or sometimes they act the opposite—using large gestures and a loud voice to attract attention, hoping to feel significant.

- Self-condemnation

Pointing out their own faults is a way for those with a low opinion of themselves to beat you to the punch, in case you noticed their long list of flaws, and they're sure you did. They often answer a compliment with, "Oh, it's nothing," or the super spiritual cover-up of "It's not me—it's the Lord at work in me," instead of a healthy "Thank you!"

- Indecision

We once knew a lady who spent twenty minutes choosing a cake mix at the market. Whether it's buying a cake or picking a college, those with poor self-esteem worry that their choices will have horrible consequences, so they often freeze when faced with a decision.

- Judgmental

Censure of others is another way people who dislike themselves try to overcome their insecurities and draw attention away from what they deem as irreparable faults. They erroneously think if they point out the toothpicks in Aunt Ginny's eye, you won't notice the logs in theirs.

- Joy-Sabotaging

Since they don't believe they deserve happiness, people who feel worthless often subconsciously undermine plans that may lead to joy. They might cancel a date to the movies with friends, not show up for their dream job interview, or refuse a marriage proposal.

- A poor self-image caused by others

Those folks in the minority who possess a healthy self-esteem might be tempted to feel superior. In that case, they need a reminder that a poor self-image is not a sign of weak faith or a flawed character. Instead, it points out some hidden wounds and deep inner pain, mostly from childhood but a few from life in general.

- A parent, teacher, or caregiver shamed, harshly criticized, or ridiculed a child or adolescent. Those memories cause deep scars on the soul that elicit feelings of inadequacy or worthlessness.
- Peers rejected or bullied a person in their growing up years. The victim mistakenly thinks they are substandard, inept, or stupid. In recent years, cyber-bullying has led to several cases of teen suicide.
- A parent abandoned or abused them as an infant or child, leading the child to believe they weren't worthy of esteem or love. Even those who've been adopted by nurturing parents may struggle into their adult years with feelings of inferiority.
- A loved one or spouse rejected someone they vowed to cherish. The abandoned one's heart may be shattered into a thousand pieces, leaving them with feelings of hopelessness and insecurity. They sometimes find it difficult to trust others, and they might develop a sarcastic outlook to cover their pain.
- A boss treated an employee poorly. Or a person has been unemployed for years, and they might doubt their worth and contribution to society.

Before we despair that our neighborhood, church, and world are nothing more than a multitude of troubled, fragile people, let's remember that God offers us abundant hope for healing. What are some of his ways to overcome a poor self-image in our own lives and offer assurance to other sufferers?

- Realize it's a process

You want to love yourself by tomorrow at five. Your friend thinks that reading one book on gaining a healthy self-esteem will fix her. But we didn't learn this unhealthy mindset in an instant, so it's going to take some time to heal. Since God is brimming with grace, he's okay with us taking baby steps of growth. With his help, we too can develop grace for ourselves for and our friends who wrestle with feelings of inferiority.

- Choose to believe God's love

When we realize that harsh treatment from others is based on lies from Satan, *the accuser of our brothers and sisters* (Rev. 12:10), that realization helps us overcome erroneous thoughts about our worth. We can refute those lies with God's Word. One counselor in a Christian home for anorexic teenagers asked the residents to make lists of their negative self-talk. Then across the page from each item on their list, they wrote truths from Scripture to renew their minds. The Bible is more powerful than every lie Satan can conceive, and its truth will set us free to believe God's love for us.

- Try journaling, art, or music therapy

The creative arts, whether guided by a trained therapist or practiced alone, can restore our emotions to health in amazing ways. As we experiment with various methods of expressing our feelings and invite the Lord alongside to heal our brokenness, we make progress toward healthier self-esteem.

- Find and encourage a natural talent

My mother-in-law once said, "I don't have any talents." Yet, she has kept meticulous records for her church's Sunday school program for decades, not realizing that a love for detail and accuracy is a gift from God. No one is without some kind of talent. It might be dog grooming, fixing cars, or cooking. As we focus on what we enjoy, we become better at those accomplishments and our self-image improves. As we encourage others' gifts, they gain self-esteem.

- Watch what we say

Mental health professionals teach a form of increasing their clients' self-image by a method called *positive affirmations*. Hearing our own voice has a powerful effect on our thinking. When we tell ourselves, "I love you. You are capable and valuable," we begin to believe it. How much more powerful for positive change when we speak God's truths over ourselves. Try personalizing these Scriptures:

- The Lord is compassionate and gracious [to me], slow to anger and abounding in love. (Psalm 103:8)
- He will take great delight in [me]; in his love he will no longer rebuke [me], but will rejoice over [me] with singing. (Zephaniah 3:17)
- The very hairs of [my] head are numbered. [I am] worth more than many sparrows. (Luke 12:7)
- But because of his great love for [me], God, who is rich in mercy, made [me] alive with Christ even when [I was]

dead in transgressions—it is by grace [I] have been saved. And God raised [me] up with Christ and seated [me] with him in the heavenly realms in Christ Jesus, in order that in the coming ages he might show the incomparable riches of his grace, expressed in his kindness to [me] in Christ Jesus. (Ephesians 2:4-7)

A champion of children and ordained minister Fred Rogers—aka Mr. Rogers—said, "If only you could sense how important you are to the lives of those you meet; how important you can be to people you may never even dream of."

Our champion of the faith, Jesus Christ said, *according to your faith let it be done to you* (Matthew 9:29).

When we focus our faith on God's view of us as precious children, our self-image changes from poor to abundant in his love and grace. Like Judy, we can like ourselves, since God so highly values us.

—Jeanette

"Rather than love, than money, than fame, give me truth."
—Henry David Thoreau

Beauty-full Thoughts
Pick one to work on this week:
____ Realize going from insecure to confident is a process.
____ Choose to believe God's love.
____ Try journaling, art, or music therapy.
____ Find and encourage a natural talent.
____ Watch what you say.

SCRIPTURES FOR MEDITATION AND ENCOURAGEMENT

Say these aloud until they take root in your heart and change the way you see yourself.

Am I now trying to win the approval of human beings, or of God? Or am I trying to please people? If I were still trying to please people, I would not be a servant of Christ. (Gal. 1:10) I am not a people-pleaser; I am a God pleaser.

The Lord will accomplish that which concerns me; Your [unwavering] lovingkindness, O Lord, endures forever—Do not abandon the works of Your own hands. (Psalm 138:8 AMP) God will not abandon me because I am the work of his hands.

He saved us, not because of any works of righteousness that we have done, but because of His own compassion and mercy, by the cleansing of the new birth (spiritual transformation, regeneration) and renewing by the Holy Spirit. (Titus 3:5 AMP). I am saved because of God's compassion and mercy toward me.

I can do all things [which He has called me to do] through Him who strengthens and empowers me [to fulfill His purpose—I am self-sufficient in Christ's sufficiency; I am ready for anything and equal to anything through Him who infuses me with inner strength and confident peace.] (Philippians 4:13 AMP) Because Jesus's strength is at work in me, I can do hard things.

Jesus Christ is the same yesterday and today and forever. (Hebrews 13:8) Since Jesus loved me before I was born, he loves me now and throughout all eternity.

And in Him you have been made complete [achieving spiritual stature through Christ], and He is the head over all rule and authority [of every angelic and earthly power]. Col. 2:10 AMP) I'm not falling apart. I am complete in Christ. He makes me significant and whole.

The Father Himself [tenderly] loves you, because you have loved Me and have believed that I came from the Father. (John 16: 27 AMP) The Father tenderly loves me because I love Jesus and believe that Jesus came from the Father.

The Lord is compassionate and gracious, slow to anger, abounding in love. He will not always accuse, nor will he harbor his anger forever; he does not treat us as our sins deserve or repay us according to our iniquities. For as high as the heavens are above the earth, so great is his love for those who fear him; as far as the east is from the west, so far has he removed our transgressions from us. As a father has compassion on his children, so the Lord has compassion on those who fear him; for he knows how we are formed, he remembers that we are dust. (Psalm 103:8-14)

As high as the heavens are above the earth, so great is God's love me. As far as the east is from the west, so far has he removed my transgressions from me. As a father has compassion on his children, so the Lord has compassion me because I fear him, for he knows how I am formed. He remembers that I am dust. Since God's love for me is unconditional and never-ending, I can and will love myself.

The Lord your God is in your midst, a warrior who saves. He will rejoice over you with joy; He will be quiet in His love [making no mention of your past sins], He will rejoice over you with shouts of joy. (Zeph. 3:17 AMP) The Lord my God is with me. He will fight for me. He takes great delight in me and rejoices over me. He will quiet me with his love.

Yet He sets the needy securely on high, away from affliction, and makes their families like a flock. (Psalm 107: 41 AMP) When I am needy and afflicted, God sets me securely on high in his arms and by his side.

Are not two sparrows sold for a penny? Yet not one of them will fall to the ground outside your Father's care. And even the very hairs of your head are all numbered. So don't be afraid; you are worth more than many sparrows. (Matt. 10:29-31). I refuse to be afraid. God loves and cares for me so much, he's even numbered the hairs of my head. I am worth more to him than all the birds of the sky.

Consider the ravens, for they neither sow nor reap; they have no storeroom nor barn, and yet God feeds them; how much more valuable you are than the birds. (Luke 12:24 NASB) If God feeds the birds, he'll definitely take care of me. I am very valuable to him.

"For the mountains may be removed and the hills may shake, but My lovingkindness will not be removed from you, nor will My covenant of peace be shaken," says the Lord who has compassion on you. (Isaiah 54:10 AMP) God's love and kindness will never leave me. I have a covenant of peace with him, and he is compassionate toward me.

"No weapon that is formed against you will succeed; and every tongue that rises against you in judgment you will condemn. This [peace, righteousness, security, and triumph over opposition] is the heritage of the servants of the Lord, And this is their vindication from Me," says the Lord. (Isaiah 54:17 AMP) The lies from Satan, put-downs from others, and my past wounds cannot succeed against me. My heritage from God is peace, right standing with God, security and triumph over opposition.

How precious to me are your thoughts, God! How vast is the sum of them! Were I to count them, they would outnumber the grains of sand—when I awake, I am still with you. (Psalm 139:17-18) God is always thinking about me. He thinks I'm precious!

Yet in all these things we are more than conquerors and gain an overwhelming victory through Him who loved us [so much that He died for us] (Romans 8:37 AMP). I'm more than a conqueror over feelings of insecurity and poor self-image through Jesus who loves me.

We have come to know and have believed the love which God has for us. God is love, and the one who abides in love abides in God, and God abides in him. (I John 4:16 NASB) I know and believe the love God has for me, and I abide—remain and live in—his love.

Therefore let us [with privilege] approach the throne of grace [that is, the throne of God's gracious favor] with confidence and without fear, so that we may receive mercy [for our failures] and find [His amazing] grace to help in time of need [an appropriate blessing, coming just at the right moment]. (Hebrews 4:16, AMP) I approach God's throne with boldness to receive mercy and grace in my time of need.

ABOUT THE AUTHORS
JEANETTE LEVELLIE

Former history teacher and newspaper columnist, spunky redhead Jeanette Levellie is the author of four published books and hundreds of articles, stories, and newspaper columns. Her writing credits include stories in *Guideposts* publications, CBN.com, *Power for Living*, and *Country* magazine. Over the last forty-plus years, she has served as a ladies' Sunday school teacher, worship leader, and women's ministry director. Jeanette is a popular speaker for a variety of audiences, including writer's conferences, women's retreats and events, church groups, and civic organizations. Her unique blend of humor and encouragement overflow in every presentation. Jeanette is active on Facebook, her blog *Hope Splashes* at www.jeanettelevelle.com, and Twitter. She makes her home in Paris, IL. with her pastor husband and three spoiled-rotten cats. She has two practically perfect grown children and three perfect grandkids. Her favorite sports are eating in restaurants, making curmudgeons laugh, and finding ways to avoid housework. www.jeanettelevellie.com

BETH GORMONG

As a past freelance copy editor for Jist Publishing and the Indiana South District of the Wesleyan Church newsletter, Beth Gormong currently works as a grant writer and freelance editor for authors. She has published devotionals in the Indiana Wesleyan University book, *From Generation to Generation*. For ten years Beth led the women's ministry at a 3000-plus member church in Terre Haute, IN, which she stepped down from to give care to her terminally ill mother. She now leads a ladies' Bible study and a *Moms in Prayer* group. She has successfully raised three grown daughters, reads the Bible from front to back every year, and loves to encourage women in their walk with Jesus. This is her first book, but not her last. Beth is active on Instagram and blogs at https://bgormong.wordpress.com/ She sells her lovely knitted creations on her Etsy shop, GreenGableStudio. Beth makes her home in Farmersburg, IN, with her husband of over twenty years and two cats. Her hobbies include knitting, gardening, and reading.

Made in the USA
Las Vegas, NV
10 May 2021